MW00416709

THE GLORY OF CHRIST

THE
GLORY
OF
CHRIST

JOHN H. ARMSTRONG
GENERAL EDITOR

CROSSWAY BOOKS

A DIVISION OF
GOOD NEWS PUBLISHERS
WHEATON, ILLINOIS

The Glory of Christ
Copyright © 2002 by John H. Armstrong
Published by Crossway Books
    A division of Good News Publishers
    1300 Crescent Street
    Wheaton, Illinois

All rights reserved. No part of this publication may be reproduced, stored in a retrieval system or transmitted in any form by any means, electronic, mechanical, photocopy, recording or otherwise, without the prior permission of the publisher, except as provided by USA copyright law.

Cover design: David LaPlaca

Unless otherwise indicated, all Scripture quotations are from *The Holy Bible, English Standard Version,* copyright © 2001 by Crossway Bibles, a division of Good News Publishers. Used by permission. All rights reserved.

Scriptures marked NIV are taken from the *Holy Bible: New International Version®.* Copyright © 1973, 1978, 1984 by International Bible Society. Used by permission of Zondervan Publishing House. All rights reserved.

The "NIV" and "New International Version" trademarks are registered in the United States Patent and Trademark Office by International Bible Society. Use of either trademark requires the permission of International Bible Society.

Scriptures marked NASB are taken from the *New American Standard Bible,* © The Lockman Foundation, 1960, 1962, 1963, 1968, 1971, 1972, 1973, 1975, 1977, 1995 and are used by permission.

Scriptures marked KJV are taken from the King James Version.

Scriptures marked *Phillips* are taken from *The New Testament in Modern English,* translated by J. B. Phillips, copyright © 1958, 1959, 1960, 1972.

First printing, 2002

Printed in the United States of America

Library of Congress Cataloging-in-Publication Data
The glory of Christ / John H. Armstrong, general editor.
    p. cm.
    Includes bibliographical references.
    ISBN 1-58134-298-5 (TPB : alk. paper)
    1. Jesus Christ—Person and offices. 2. Revivals—United States.
3. Reformed Church—United States—Doctrines. I. Armstrong, John H.
(John Harper) 1949-
BT202.G565   2002
232—dc21   2002003047
                                           CIP

15	14	13	12	11	10	09	08	07	06	05	04	03	02
15	14	13	12	11	10	9	8	7	6	5	4	3	2	1

*For the reformation of the church and the revival of
biblical Christianity in an increasingly dark time
in history when integrity in both life and doctrine
is the crying need of evangelical Christianity.*

*And for
Pastor Thomas N. Smith,
who preaches the glory of Christ with as much clarity
and biblical fidelity as any minister I know and
is the definition of a true friend who becomes
more dear to my soul with every passing day.
Your patient, prophetic, and wise counsel
immeasurably benefits my life and labors.*

TABLE OF CONTENTS

ACKNOWLEDGMENTS

THE GENERAL EDITOR would like to thank the board of Reformation & Revival Ministries, Inc., for their support and faithful friendship in the work that Christ has given to me as His servant. Each of these board members actively gives time, talent, and money to make my ministry possible—Bruce Bickel, Jerry Kamphuis, Wendell Hawley, Richard Johnson, Irv Queal, Andy Froiland, Charles McGowen, Mark Coppenger, Wilbur Ellsworth, Kurt Klippert, David Melvin, and Robert Mulder.

Thanks to my faithful staff—Wendell Hawley, Stacy Armstrong, Steve Board, Tim Campbell, Horst Fiebig, Anita Armstrong, and Robert Mulder. In addition I have been greatly helped by the special assistance of two men who currently serve me in the expanding work of Reformation & Revival to pastors and church leadership—Luder Whitlock and T. M. Moore. Thanks, brothers and sisters, for giving so much to help a work that we believe God has given to us.

As always my greatest appreciation goes to Anita, my wife of nearly thirty-two years. You have once again helped me to stay the course, to do my work day in and day out, and to finish this project with great joy. Thanks in particular for your editorial efforts on this particular book. Your skills in both editing and English grammar aid me wonderfully. Without your human encouragement, spiritual support, and sunny disposition I am not sure I could have pressed on during times of physical weakness and trial over the past four years. Without the slightest doubt it should be said of you: "Her children rise up and call her blessed; *her husband also, and he praises her*" (Prov. 31:28, emphasis added).

Thanks again to Dr. Lane Dennis. You are a publisher who combines courage and integrity with grace and love. Thanks also to Marvin Padgett who brings great zeal and vision to Christian publishing. You both had the foresight and conviction to publish a book on the glory of the Lord Jesus Christ in a time when few publishers, sadly, are willing to do so.

This book grew out of an annual national conference on reformation and revival, held in October 2000 at College Church in Wheaton, Illinois. It is in order, therefore, to say a word of thanks to Dr. R. Kent Hughes, who graciously supported our ministry in this event and who has been my pastor for over ten years. Thanks for praying for me, Kent, and for your personal concern for my ministry for nearly twenty-five years.

Finally, a word of thanks is in order for the three other contributors to this volume. You men have all worked diligently to complete your task, and you have proven to be Christian gentlemen in the process. I thank you and pray with you that your written work will now be a blessing to many.

My prayer is that the glory of Christ will shine brightly again in the lives of a multitude of Christians. This book is aimed at that purpose with the hope that it might be one more log on a fire of true revival. If this book contributes something to this end, the four who contributed will be profoundly delighted.

THE CONTRIBUTORS

GENERAL EDITOR

John H. Armstrong (B.A., M.A., Wheaton College; D. Min., Luther Rice Seminary) is founder and president of Reformation & Revival Ministries in Carol Stream, Illinois. He served as a pastor for twenty-one years before becoming a conference speaker and editor of *Reformation & Revival Journal* (a quarterly publication for church leadership) and *Viewpoint* (a bimonthly magazine for the church). He is the general editor of the books *Reforming Pastoral Ministry, Roman Catholicism: Evangelical Protestants Analyze What Unites & Divides Us, The Coming Evangelical Crisis: Current Challenges to the Authority of Scripture and the Gospel*, and *The Compromised Church: The Present Evangelical Crisis*. He is author of *The Stain That Stays: The Problem of Fallen Pastoral Leadership, The Catholic Mystery, True Revival: What Happens When God Moves*, and *Five Great Evangelists*. He serves as a theological consultant to several ministries and has contributed to numerous books and periodicals. He also directly assists congregations in biblical reformation and travels internationally in a conference-speaking ministry.

OTHER CONTRIBUTORS

Jim Elliff (B.A., Ouachita Baptist University; M. Div., Southwestern Baptist Theological Seminary) is president of Christian Communicators Worldwide and a consultant for the Midwestern

Center for Biblical Revival at Midwestern Baptist Theological
Seminary, Kansas City, Missouri. He is the author of numerous
booklets distributed through Christian Communicators
Worldwide and regularly contributes to various publications. He
is the author of *Led by the Spirit*.

R. *Albert Mohler, Jr.* (B.A., Samford University; M.Div.,
Ph.D., Southern Baptist Theological Seminary) serves as the ninth
president of Southern Baptist Theological Seminary. Formerly
the editor of *The Christian Index*, he was general editor for *Gods
of the Age or God of the Ages?* He was also a contributor *to The
Compromised Church* (Crossway Books, 1998). Dr. Mohler was
named one of *Time* magazine's most promising leaders age forty
and under in the December 5, 1994, issue.

James I. Packer (D. Phil., Oxford University) is Board of
Governors' Professor of Theology at Regent College, Vancouver,
British Columbia. An ordained minister in the Church of England,
he was warden of Latimer House (Oxford) and the principal of
Tyndale Hall. He presently serves as an executive editor of
Christianity Today and is a frequent contributor to numerous the-
ological periodicals. Among his books are *Evangelism and the
Sovereignty of God, I Want to Be a Christian, Your Father Loves
You, Rediscovering Holiness, God's Words, Keep in Step with
the Spirit, Beyond the Battle for the Bible, Hot Tub Religion, A
Passion for Faithfulness, A Quest for Godliness, Concise
Theology, Great Grace, Great Power, Great Joy, A Grief
Sanctified*, and the best seller *Knowing God*. He served as editor
of *the New Bible Dictionary, The Bible Almanac*, and *The New
Dictionary of Theology*. He also served as chairman of the trans-
lation committee for the English Standard Version.

EDITOR'S PREFACE

JOHN H. ARMSTRONG

SEVERAL DECADES AGO the famous minister and author A. W. Tozer wrote: "Jesus Christ today has almost no authority at all among the groups that call themselves by his name. . . . I [refer to] Protestant churches generally, especially those who protest the loudest that they are in spiritual descent from our Lord and his apostles: the evangelicals." Not much has changed since Tozer wrote these words, except that his observation is more *obviously* true now.

The Bible is preached, in many of our conservative churches, as if its purpose is to be a handbook for daily living, a guide for a happy marriage or for successful child rearing. We continually look to God for principles and insights. We would be more in line with the revealed purpose of Holy Scripture if we looked for fresh revelations of the person of God's unique Son, Jesus Christ. Moral examples and lessons in civility abound throughout popular evangelicalism. But where is the preaching of the Christ of the Bible? Indeed, is not the central and eternal purpose of Holy Scripture to reveal to us, by the witness and power of the Holy Spirit, the wonder of Christ alone?

Jesus rebuked a similar group of conservative people in His own day when He said, "You search the Scriptures because you think that in them you have eternal life; and it is they that bear witness about me, yet you refuse to come to me that you may have life" (John 5:39-40). The whole focus of the Bible is upon Jesus Christ, from Genesis to Revelation; yet the modern emphasis is upon church growth, self-esteem, political activism, codependency, and a host of related "practical" issues that have replaced the preaching and worship of Christ in the contemporary church.

This book was prepared in view of this present problem and with the purpose of addressing that need by helping the church recover her vision of the wonder of Christ alone! The Reformers of the sixteenth century underscored this same emphasis by the slogan *solus Christus*—Christ alone! It is not too much to say that modern reformation and true revival will never come until we recover the centrality of Jesus Christ in the hearts of God's own people. To make Christ alone the focus of every believer and church in America should be much more than a sixteenth-century slogan. It should represent the only goal worth pursuing by those of us who truly love the church.

Those who have contributed to this present volume, *The Glory of Christ*, all prayerfully submit their thoughts with the hope that this book might be one small piece in a new twenty-first-century reformation that we pray shall soon be ignited.

1

SOLUS CHRISTUS:
THE WONDER OF CHRIST'S GLORY

JOHN H. ARMSTRONG

FOR OVER THIRTY YEARS I have been a student of revival move-
ments. As a result of this passion and study I am frequently asked,
"What do you think is happening spiritually in America in these
tumultuous times? Is there a great move of God's Spirit going on,
or is all this intense spiritual interest something else?" In the light
of the tragic events of September 11, 2001, many have wondered,
"Are Americans *really* turning to God in a new way?" The evidence of several national polls suggests a negative answer. Several
years ago *U.S. News & World Report*[1] ran a rather amazing editorial that touched on this very question in a most interesting way.
The title of this perceptive editorial was, "Divining the God
Factor: Are Americans Really Undergoing a Spiritual Revival?" I
draw three observations from this unusually clearheaded piece.

First, if there is anything to be said about the present religious situation in North America it is this: We seem to have spent
centuries of moral and religious capital in a few decades. Only
the remnants of a once great civilization remain. Second, we have
already tried, at least for a time, to create a culture that gets rid

of God altogether. Third, since this effort to get rid of God has
miserably failed we are now turning, as did pagan peoples before
us, to "new" gods, "new" divinities, and "new" worldviews.
You can hear the theologies of these new gods every day on the
modern televised equivalents of the ancient Mars Hill—e.g., talk
radio, cable channel interviews, and of course the *Oprah* TV
program. This same direction can also be witnessed in the countless new *spiritualities* that appear almost weekly. These are not
even remotely Christian. From firsthand observation, I can tell you
that all of these also permeate the Christian church in every region
of the country.

One is almost tempted to say, "Woe to the person who tries
to find a worship setting in a modern church that actually culti-
vates the glory of the *transcendent* God!" We have clearly lost
our way. We have searched for God, but as David Wells has often
put it, the god we have found is "no longer morally angular." To
use the language of the Bible, in our culture we have "exchanged
the truth about God for a lie" and thus now "worship[ed] and
serve[d] the creature rather than the Creator" (Rom. 1:25). The
result is moral chaos and the rise of a coming generation of moral
degenerates whose energy and lifestyle will soon permeate the
wider society with an even greater leavening effect. In the church
the situation is not much better; here we find ecclesial confusion,
moral chaos, and endless wars about worship style, evangelism,
and church growth.

It was not always this way. The Protestant Reformation of
the sixteenth century was, if nothing else, a divinely sparked
awakening that was profoundly centered upon the glory of God.
And this glory was clearly centered in the person of Jesus Christ.
Consider, as an example of this point, words of the Genevan
reformer John Calvin, from several of his commentaries.

> The proclaiming of God's glory on earth . . . is the very end of
> our existence.[2]

God is called jealous, because he permits no rivalry that may detract from his glory.[3]

There is scarcely one among a hundred who makes the manifestation of God's glory his chief end.[4]

Calvin, writing in his commentary on Isaiah, further noted that, "the Church [was] the principal theatre of his glory."[5] This is not exactly the view most evangelicals have about the church in our generation. But what do we mean by "the glory of God"? The words sound so foreign to modern self-affirming Christians.

In the Old Testament the most direct and dramatic manifestation of God (Yahweh) displayed, above all else, His holiness. God is preeminently a holy being. God's holiness and majesty are the very essence of the divine glory. This was exactly what was most often revealed in the fire of light (as to Moses) or in the fiery presence surrounded by a cloud that looked something like smoke. This fire, this blinding light and dense cloud in which Yahweh appeared, was the *Shekinah*. The *Shekinah* was the revelation of the glory of almighty God Himself.

By the time of the sixteenth century this biblical sense of the glory of God, as found preeminently in the person of Christ, had been lost to the Christian church. The glory was understood in a completely different way in that century. It was looked for in church ceremonies, in drama, in the priesthood, and most prominently in the church's sacramental system, which was designed to fill the human tank with divine grace for the long journey that hopefully led the faithful person to heaven.

The Protestant Reformation changed all this in a most profound way. If nothing else, at least for a time, scores of ministers and ordinary Christians saw once again that the whole Christian life was to be consciously centered in the glory of God through faith in Christ alone. This understanding of the revelation of divine glory was what the Reformers meant by "the glory of

Christ." Thus they spoke of Christ alone, or *solus Christus*—one of the great watchwords of the reform movement.

The principal figures of the era—Martin Luther, Philipp Melanchthon, Ulrich Zwingli, Martin Bucer, and John Calvin— all celebrated this reality, the glory of Christ. The central theological struggles of their time were not about indulgences, the number and nature of the sacraments, the papacy, or even *finally* about the place of grace and faith. I need to explain what I mean.

The Reformers understood that the Old Testament prepared the way for Christ. Its central message was the unfolding account of the glory of Yahweh, to be finally revealed at a definite historical point in the redemptive purpose of God. The New Testament told of Christ's birth, life, death, resurrection, ascension, and future coming again. At the center of the whole of Scripture these Reformers saw a person—namely, one person, the God-man, Christ Jesus. And at the center of this one person's life story was one primary purpose—to bring glory to God in the salvation of a people.

Just as surely as the material principles of the Reformation were grounded in *sola gratia* and *sola fide* (and the formal principle in *sola Scriptura*), so these great truths made no real sense without this central emphasis of the entire movement—*solus Christus*. But why?

Just as the great Reformation text, "The righteous shall live by faith" (Rom. 1:17), drove Martin Luther to rely entirely upon the righteousness of God for his redemption, so the entire body of Protestant Reformers understood that "faith alone" plainly meant "faith in Christ alone." Thus, in a very real sense the person of Christ was the necessity behind the doctrinal formulations of *sola gratia* and *sola fide*. By this I mean that these truths were ultimately important precisely because the Reformers came to recover the glorious truth that Christ was the central figure of human history. They delighted in the fact that Christ was the theme of divine revelation. And they believed, and put into practice, the truth that Christ should be the subject of true preaching.

Think about this theologically for a moment. Grace alone demands that God alone saves sinners. God does this solely by the provision of His Son. *Faith alone* must mean, if it has any true biblical meaning and is not emptied of divine wisdom, that salvation consists in clinging to Christ alone to save us. Faith, understood properly, is complete reliance upon, or total trust in, Jesus Christ alone. And this living Christ is the living Word, revealed to me by the Spirit of God through the Holy Scriptures. Stated quite simply this means: God alone rescues sinners on the basis of Christ's life and death alone!

The purposes of God for this age, and for all ages to come, are to be found in Christ alone. He is the Alpha and the Omega. The hopes and fears of every seeking soul are found in the God-man, Jesus of Nazareth. Francis Scott Key, the author of America's "National Anthem," wrote several Christian hymns. One such hymn captures well this sense of the glory of Yahweh as found in Christ alone.

> *Lord, with glowing heart I'd praise Thee*
> *for the bliss Thy love bestows.*
> *For the pardoning grace that saves me,*
> *and the peace that from it flows;*
> *Help, O God, my weak endeavor;*
> *this dull soul to rapture raise:*
> *Thou must light the flame, or never*
> *can my love be warmed to praise.*

> *Praise my soul, the God that sought thee,*
> *wretched wanderer far astray;*
> *Found thee lost, and kindly brought thee*
> *from the paths of death away:*
> *Praise, with love's devoutest feeling,*
> *Him who saw thy guilt-born fear,*
> *And, the light of hope revealing,*
> *bade the bloodstained cross appear.*

Praise thy Saviour God that drew thee
  to that cross, new life to give,
Held a blood-sealed pardon to thee,
  bade thee look to him and live:
Praise the grace whose threats alarmed thee,
  roused thee from thy fatal ease,
Praise the grace whose promise warmed thee,
  praise the grace that whispered peace.

Lord, this bosom's ardent feeling
  vainly would my lips express;
Low before Thy footstool kneeling,
  deign Thy suppliant's prayer to bless:
Let Thy love, my soul's chief treasure,
  love's pure flame within me raise;
And since words can never measure,
  let my life show forth Thy praise.[6]

Simply put, in all of Holy Scripture Christ is preeminent. Nowhere is this seen more clearly than in Paul's letter to the Colossians. This is especially true in chapter 1. Here you can see how Paul reaches back, as well as forward, to express the absolute supremacy of Christ. There are three amazing paragraphs in this long statement. From verse 9 through verse 20 there are 218 words, which form one complete sentence. The subject of the entire epistle is captured in this very long sentence—the glory of the person and work of Jesus Christ!

Make no mistake, the supremacy of Christ has been challenged for nearly two thousand years. From the beginning, both Jews and Gentiles (Romans and Greeks) challenged the sovereign reign of Christ, both politically and religiously. Many Jews refused to embrace Him as their Messiah. A remnant did receive Him for who He was—the *new* temple, the *new* Moses, the *new* Israel, the *true* sovereign who fulfilled *all* the promises and religious symbols that Yahweh had given to His ancient people Israel.

This is why Paul wrote as he did to this little flock in Colossae. Their nascent faith was under direct attack. This attack, as has so often been the case through the years, came from *within* the church. This challenge arose again from within the church in the fourth and fifth centuries, and yet again in the nineteenth and twentieth. In the sixteenth century the centrality of Christ was challenged in a much more subtle way. A religious system existed in the late medieval church that kept men and women from coming *directly* to Christ as their Savior.

This situation led the sixteenth-century Protestant Reformers to use two Latin words, *solus Christus*, to describe a central truth that was needed to reform the church in faith and practice—*solus*, used as an adjective, and *Christus*, used as a reference to the Messiah, who was literally "the anointed one." The Latinized version of the Greek *Christos* refers to Christ's *nomen officii*, or his official name in terms of His office as the Mediator. The idea behind *solus Christus*, then, was basic and most important to the recovery that was ongoing at the time. Christ alone, as the divinely anointed mediator, saved the one who trusted in Him. Thus Christ was, in their evangelical theology, the theme, the glory, and the sole redeemer of the world. This is exactly what Paul is saying in Colossians chapter 1—Christ is all-glorious!

THE GLORY OF CHRIST IS SEEN IN CREATION

In his letter Paul responds to several ancient errors in Colossae. Chapter 2 provides an example. Here he corrects several Jewish errors regarding Christ. Contrary to popular interpretations, these errors do not appear to me to have been Gnostic. Paul insists throughout this little epistle that Christ is central. Christ alone is able to grant the prayer that Paul prayed for these believers in 1:9-14:

> And so, from the day we heard, we have not ceased to pray for
> you, asking that you may be filled with the knowledge of his will
> in all spiritual wisdom and understanding, so as to walk in a
> manner worthy of the Lord, fully pleasing to him, bearing fruit
> in every good work and increasing in the knowledge of God.

May you be strengthened with all power, according to his glo-
rious might, for all endurance and patience with joy, giving
thanks to the Father, who has qualified you to share in the inher-
itance of the saints in light. He has delivered us from the domain
of darkness and transferred us to the kingdom of his beloved
Son, in whom we have redemption, the forgiveness of sins.

If *Christ alone* can do all of this, then it is not hard to understand why we do not need additional help before the throne of
God. This is why the Reformers rejected dependence upon Mary,
the saints, the hierarchy of the visible church, and even mystical
experience.

The poetic form of Colossians 1, especially in verses 15-20,
is generally considered to be one of the most important
Christological statements of the entire New Testament. The most
obvious point the poem makes is that there is a parallel between
creation and *new* creation; hence the emphasis is placed upon
the fact that both creative acts were accomplished by the same
agent—Jesus Christ.

The glory is seen in this: In His essence Christ is God of very
God (v. 15). He is the "image of the invisible God." He is the
perfect representation of the Father. The Son differs from the
essence of the Father in no particular. Christ is the one "in whom
are hidden all the treasures of wisdom and knowledge" (2:3), as
well as the one in whom "the whole fullness of deity dwells bodily" (2:9). Simply put, He is the perfect manifestation of the
Father; the nature and being of God are perfectly manifested in
Him. Thus John writes, "No one has ever seen God; the only God,
who is at the Father's side, he has made him known" (John 1:18).

The modern New Testament scholar N. T. Wright has
expressed this quite clearly:

From all eternity Jesus had, in his very nature, been the "image
of God," reflecting perfectly the character and life of the
Father. It was thus appropriate for him to be the "image of

God" as man: from all eternity he had held the same relation to the Father that humanity, from its creation, had been intended to bear. Humanity was designed to be the perfect vehicle for God's self-expression within this world, so that he could himself live appropriately among his people as one of themselves, could rule in love over creation as himself a creature. God made us for himself, as Augustine said with a different, though perhaps related, meaning. The doctrine of incarnation that flows from this cannot, by definition, squeeze either "divinity" or "humanity" out of shape. Indeed, it is only in Jesus Christ that we understand what "divinity" and "humanity" really mean: without him, we lapse into sub-Christian, or even pagan, categories of thought, and then wonder why the doctrine of incarnation causes us so much difficulty. Paul's way of expressing the doctrine is to say, poetically, that the man Jesus fulfills the purposes which God had marked out both for himself and for humanity.[7]

THE GLORY OF CHRIST IS SEEN IN HIS RELATIONSHIP TO THE WORLD AS ITS SOVEREIGN

Paul refers to Christ as "the firstborn of all creation" (v. 15). If the term "image" tells us of the *essence* of Christ, then "firstborn" relates to His position in the created order. (The NIV correctly uses the term "over," not "of.") But what is in view in this statement? Does Paul mean that Jesus is the first *created being* in God's creation? Well, this is exactly what various heresies have claimed through the centuries. Arius argued, "There was a time when he was not!" But the high Christology of the apostle will not allow such an idea if the text is properly read. Is the right way to read this passage to see Christ as the image of the invisible God by virtue of His *becoming flesh*?

I suggest that the idea that Christ is the first created being cannot be true since in the immediate context Paul is plainly saying that Christ is Himself the Creator! The term "firstborn" refers to someone who is *first in rank* or one who has the rights of an heir; i.e., He is the sovereign over all creation. Furthermore, *eter-*

nal preexistence refutes the notion (v. 17). In addition, the New
Testament plainly refutes such an idea elsewhere.

> *In the beginning was the Word, and the Word was with God,*
> *and the Word was God. He was in the beginning with God.*
> *All things were made through him, and without him was not*
> *any thing made that was made.*
>
> —JOHN 1:1-3

A very strong verb is used in John's prologue that has the
idea of coming into being. The conclusion is obviously clear.
Jesus cannot be reduced to a product of history since John is
plainly saying history is the product of Christ's sovereign activity. Paul's words are in perfect agreement with those of the Gospel
writer John.

THE GLORY IS TO BE SEEN IN TERMS OF WHAT IS (CREATION)—CHRIST MADE EVERYTHING

> *For by him all things were created, in heaven and on earth,*
> *visible and invisible, whether thrones or dominions or rulers*
> *or authorities—all things were created through him and for*
> *him.*
>
> —COL. 1:16

What an array of prepositions the apostle uses in this verse.
First he says, "*by* him all things were created, in heaven and on
earth"; that is, *within the sphere of His power* all that exists came
into being. The "by" (*dia*; i.e., through) makes explicit the fact
that everything came *through* Him, and thus Jesus is the agent of
all creation. For this reason He has absolute and total dominion.
Further, everything that was made was made "for" Him—He is
the end for which everything exists. Not only is He the sphere
and the agency of everything created, but He is the goal—the
end! Jesus Christ is prior to, distinct from, and highly exalted over
every other creature in the entire universe. Nothing exists that
He doesn't have authority over—absolutely nothing!

THE GLORY OF CHRIST IS REVEALED BY THE FACT THAT THE CREATION IS CURRENTLY SUSTAINED BY HIM

But this is not all. Paul adds: "And he is before all things, and in him all things hold together" (1:17). Many seem to think that God created everything and then simply withdrew into a small corner of the universe. This infers that God says, "My hands are off now—the created order and its direction is now out of My control. Let's see what these created beings will do with it." Such an idea says in effect, "Yes, God is the sovereign," but then when it comes to defining His dominion and rule it qualifies it severely. You can hear a repeated refrain in this type of thinking: "But . . . but . . . but . . ." (This prompted a friend of mine to humorously call this "Billy Goat Theology" with its continual refrain of "but this" and "but that.")

"Before all things" (v. 17) means Christ was preexistent. "In him all things hold together." That means He keeps and sustains everything that exists. If Christ presently holds all things together, then His involvement in this world is not passive, whatever else you might say. The writer of Hebrews rightly insists that Christ now "upholds the universe by the word of his power" (Heb. 1:3). This Colossian text is a typically Jewish form of monotheism, which makes a strong statement against any kind of dualism that sees creation as bad. The *form* throughout this passage is Jewish; the *context* is clearly Christ!

Do you begin to grasp the mystery and glory of a Christ-centered faith? Without revelation from God you would never know this truth; yet with this revelation you can never plumb the depths of Christ's majesty and glory. If He is supreme over all that is, and if He sustains everything that is in His sovereign power, then we should be directly impacted by this reality. So we see that the glory of Yahweh is *fully* and *finally* revealed in Christ alone. We must more fully recognize the Christocentric nature of our world. For this reason there can be no *meaningful* distinction between secular and sacred if we truly do all for the glory of Christ.

THE GLORY OF CHRIST IS REVEALED IN HIS RELATIONSHIP TO THE CHURCH

The point made here is that Christ has ecclesiastical preeminence. A perfect exposition of this idea occurs in a familiar hymn written by Samuel Stone:

> *The church's one foundation is Jesus Christ her Lord;*
> *She is his new creation by water and the word;*
> *From heaven he came and sought her to be his holy bride;*
> *With his own blood he bought her, and for her life he died.*

Regarding the church there are four things said in Colossians 1 regarding Christ's dominion.

First, we read, "He is the head of the body" (v. 18). He is the church's potentate and ruler. Indeed, we can properly say that He alone is the *senior pastor* of the church. In this verse, in the careful structure of this poem, Paul's thought moves from the physical creation to the new creation. The Colossian believers must understand that they are members of the one-world people of God. God's people are the new humanity, and hence they have a dependent relationship upon Christ as their "head." (Paul mixes his metaphors freely, as you will see if you pay careful attention to the words here.)

But is Paul referring to the church here as a *local congregation* or a *universal reality*? I believe New Testament scholar Peter O'Brien is correct in the way he answers this question:

> Certainly local gatherings are not part of the heavenly church any more than they are part of an alleged universal church. Paul consistently refers to the church that meets in a particular place. Even when there are several gatherings in a single city (e.g., at Corinth) the individual assemblies are not understood as part of the church in that place. This suggests that each of the various local churches are manifestations of the heavenly church, tangible expressions in time and space of what is heavenly and eternal.[8]

I think I first heard Michael Griffiths, many years ago, refer to this as "the universal church in local circumscription." I like that phrase. It is much more faithful to the New Testament than some of our modern notions that treat the church as if it were an option. I can illustrate this idea by the moon. When the moon is half full or a quarter full, we say, on a clear night when we can see the stellar heavens, "There is the moon." We do not say, "There is a *half* moon" or "There is a *quarter* moon." We understand that we see only part of the whole, but what we see is still the moon. The same is true when you see a local church. It is not a *half* church but the church of Jesus Christ in that place.

Second, the apostle adds, "He is the beginning" (v. 18)—the *archē* (literally, "the origin"). N. T. Wright is helpful once again. He observes that Paul has been exploring the different meanings of the Hebrew *reshith* ("firstborn" or "head") and now reaches a *final stage* in his exploration.[9] There is no "and" in the Greek text here.

Third, we read that Christ is "the firstborn from the dead" (v. 18). That means He is the first to conquer death. Because He conquered death, so shall we, by virtue of our union with Him who is "the firstborn from the dead." The use of the word "beginning" in verse 18 is not clear enough in English. What is said, literally, is that Christ is *first principle*, the *creative initiative* of everything that now exists. But what is the point?

Paul is plainly referring to Christ's rule over the final great enemies of mankind—the rule of sin and death. In Christ's death and resurrection the new age has dawned. The future has actually broken into the present. The curse has been reversed in Christ's person and work, and He is now actively leading everything to its appointed end, in Himself and by his prerogative. Indeed, what we see here is "Back to the Future" in the fullest sense.

Throughout the Bible sin and death are inextricably linked,

and so Christ's victory over death signaled His defeat of sin. This is the idea behind two very important Christological texts—Romans 5:12-21 and 1 Corinthians 15:12-28. Christ's great victory, though presently *unique* to Him, is the "first" or the "beginning" of a large-scale company of victories to come.

What we have here is Pauline eschatology. The Jews—certainly the Pharisees and likely others as well—looked forward to a great resurrection event at the end of time. What Paul says, I believe, is that God brought the *age to come* (the age of resurrection) forward into this *present age*. He did this through and in Christ alone. And by this one act of Christ, the power of the new age is now being unleashed in this present world.

Finally, at the very end of verse 18, Christ is said to have first place in everything; He has complete supremacy. What Christ was through divine right—namely, supreme—He has *become* in actual human history. This is the revelation of His resplendent glory. This alone will ultimately move us to awe, to worship, and to holy, Christ-centered living. I think I comfortably can say that the church desperately needs this vision in every age. It especially needs this in the present age when everything indicates that our focus is quite clearly elsewhere.

Please observe that God is not merely working all things together for His purpose *within the old creation*. What He has actually done is begin a *whole new creation*. What Christ was before His resurrection is now given public preeminence. N. T. Wright aptly concludes, "The puzzle is caused by sin: though always Lord by right, he must become Lord in fact, by defeating sin and death."[10]

Jesus was "Son of God" as well as "descended from David according to the flesh" *before* His resurrection. But by His resurrection these facts are powerfully demonstrated in a *public* manner (Rom. 1:3-4), and the victory of His reign breaks into the present.

THE GLORY OF CHRIST IS SEEN IN RECONCILIATION

For in him all the fullness of God was pleased to dwell, and through him to reconcile to himself all things, whether on earth or in heaven, making peace by the blood of his cross.
—COL. 1:19-20

Paul now explains why the truth he has written in verse 18 is appropriate. Here we are brought face to face with one of the most difficult and amazing texts regarding the work of Christ in all the New Testament.

Notice how effortlessly Paul passes from Christ's person to His work—no separation is allowable (see 2 Cor. 5:19, "in Christ God was reconciling the world to himself"). God, in all His fullness, was pleased to take up permanent residence in Christ. This is quite startling. There are not two divinities—Yahweh and Jesus. Yahweh, the God of Israel, has taken up residence in Jesus of Nazareth. "In him all the fullness of God was pleased to dwell."

It appears that the text is saying Christ *will* reconcile or *already has* reconciled everything to God *through* His cross! (The words are *ta panta*—"all things.") This, in fact, is precisely what Origen taught in the third century. Erasmus, the great humanist scholar of the sixteenth century, even said that *all* the angels were reconciled to God. On an elemental level this text is saying what Romans 8 says regarding creation and redemption:

For I consider that the sufferings of this present time are not worth comparing with the glory that is to be revealed to us. For the creation waits with eager longing for the revealing of the sons of God. For the creation was subjected to futility, not willingly, but because of him who subjected it, in hope that the creation itself will be set free from its bondage to decay and obtain the freedom of the glory of the children of God.
—ROM. 8:18-21

But what is this "things . . . in heaven" business in Colossians 1:20? The answer is found by keeping in mind the meaning of reconciliation—*the removal of all hostility.* There are two ways to accomplish such removal. First, by grace and through the overtures of mercy accepted. Second, by subjugation (cf. 2:15). What Paul is saying is this: Christ's work on the cross had both the goal and purpose of removing all hostility and enmity, totally and finally!

The "all things" should be understood in terms of three further questions. First, how does the death of Jesus *effect* reconciliation between God and humankind?

There is no real problem in answering this question. On the cross Jesus took upon Himself sin and death. The worst that sin can do, it already did to Him: It kills!

Notice *how* He accomplished this—"by the blood of his cross" (cf. 2 Cor. 5:21 and Col. 1:22; 2:11-15). But does the expression "all things" refer to nonhuman creation? To put this another way, what is the actual scope of this new creation?

The point is fairly straightforward. Just as human sin impacted the whole world, so human reconciliation will have a *worldwide impact* (Rom. 8:19). The cosmic outworking of the implications of the cross is presently going forward in this world. Someday it will reach its final stage. But will all human beings finally be saved? The clearest conclusion that we are warranted to make is that there will be universal reconciliation, but not universal salvation for all persons (cf. Rom. 1:18—2:16; 14:10; 2 Cor. 5:10; etc.).

It seems to me two things are going on in this text. First, Paul is emphasizing the *universal scope* of God's reconciling purposes—i.e., a total new creation is in view!

If a mutual relationship between God and man is to be established, then this takes place (2 Cor. 5:17) only when we are "*in* Christ." This means all rebellion has been settled. It was settled two thousand years ago outside the city walls of Jerusalem. All that happens now are mini-rebellions, all of which will be put down in the end. (For this reason we should not say, "Satan is alive and well on planet earth," but rather, "Satan has been stripped of all authority and openly routed by King Jesus on planet earth!")

You must either run to Christ, who alone has all dominion, and to his cross, where mercy is to be found, or you will face his judgment without hope in the Last Day. This much is clearly declared in our text—your rebellion, my rebellion, all cosmic rebellion, has been defeated by the supremacy and glory of Christ.

CONCLUSION

There are two very crucial things we should understand about the glory of Christ from these observations.

First, all the fullness of God is in Jesus Christ, and thus new reformations and revivals will break forth in our present age when He is glorified in His people. Consider the implications for the future glory yet to come.

We reckon far too infrequently upon these startling facts. We do think about the Protestant Reformation, as well as past revivals and awakenings. But when we reckon upon these we often do so only as *past* facts and *past* glories. C. H. Spurgeon provides wonderful counsel at this point.

> "We have heard with our ears, and our fathers have told us the wondrous things which thou didst in their day and in the old time before them," but we dolefully complain that the golden age of Christianity is over, its heroic times are a matter of history. Indeed, this feeling is transformed to fact, for scarcely any church now existing realizes that it can do what its first promoters did, all appear to be quite sure that these are bad times and but little is to be done in them. We do not expect now-a-days to find a Methodist so full of fire as the first field-preachers, the Quakers are never fanatical, and even the Primitives are not Ranters now; the old reproach has ceased because the old ardour which provoked it has cooled down. So far so bad. I see grave cause of sorrow in this. A people are in an evil case when all their heroism is historical. We read the biographies of former worthies with great wonder and respect,

but we do not attempt to follow in their steps with equal stride. Wherefore not? It has pleased the Father that in Jesus all the fulness should *dwell*, a fulness for Paul, a fulness for Luther, a fulness for Whitefield, and blessed be God, a fulness for me, and a fulness for you. All that Jesus has given forth has not exhausted him. Christianity has not lost its pristine strength; we have lost our faith, there's the calamity. . . . The fulness of Jesus is not changed; then why are our works so feebly done? Pentecost, is that a tradition? The reforming days, are these to be memories only? I see no reason why we should not have a greater Pentecost than Peter saw, and a Reformation deeper in its foundations, and truer in its upbuildings than all the reforms Luther or Calvin achieved. We have the same Christ, remember that. The times are altered, but Jesus is the Eternal, and time touches him not. "But we are not such men as they." What, then, cannot God make us such? Are we weaker than they? The fitter to be instruments for the mighty God. Out with the cowardice which thinks the past is never to be outdone. We must labour to eclipse the past as the sunlight eclipses the brightness of the stars.

Furthermore, our churches believe that there is a great fulness in Christ, and that sometimes they ought to enjoy it. The progress of Christianity is to be by tides which ebb and flow. There are to be revivals like the spring, and these must alternate with long lethargies like the winter. Accursed unbelief, wilt thou always pervert the truth? Wilt thou never understand this word, "It pleased the Father that in him should all the fulness dwell"? It is not the Lord's purpose that fulness should reside in Jesus during revivals, and then withdraw. Jesus Christ is the same yesterday, today and forever. The highest state of revival should be the normal condition of the church. When her martyrs are most self-sacrificing, her missionaries most daring, her ministers most bold, her members most consecrated, she is even then below her standard, she has not fully reached her high calling; to come down from her position would be sin. God grant us grace to feel that we have not to drink of an intermittent spring, nor to work for Christ with an occasional industry, but as all the fulness *dwells* in him, it is ours to believe that today we can have all the blessing of a true revival, that today we can go forward in the power of God, that at this very hour we lack for nothing which can lift the church into her highest condition of spirituality and power. God grant us to receive grace for today.[11]

Second, these extraordinary events of Christ's incarnation and cross were not undertaken with any reluctance.

Observe this glory more closely. God's hands were never tied. Consider again verse 19. God was "pleased," says Paul. This is utterly amazing. He was pleased! God actually took pleasure in doing this. Psalm 68:16 says that Yahweh is *pleased* to dwell on Mount Zion. Paul says that God is now *pleased* "to dwell" among His people. And the fourth Gospel says, "And the Word became flesh and dwelt among us, and we have seen his glory, glory as of the only Son from the Father, full of grace and truth" (John 1:14).

In a world that has rejected certainty and absolutes, Christians have one Absolute, the person and work of our glorious Jesus Christ. Our world is increasingly questioning monotheism and is racing for modalities and spiritualities that are clearly opposed to Christ. But this glory, His glory, will outshine all other glories. When the church sees this glory with fresh eyes and hearts, she will be awakened to new exploits of faith, hope, and love.

There is truth to be seen in other philosophies and religions for sure. (Colossians 1:16 even allows this, I think, since it says all creation came from Him.) But there is only *one* person and *one* way into the new creation. The glory of God is seen in Isaiah 6:3: "Holy, holy, holy is the Lord of hosts; the whole earth is full of his glory." We must understand that this is not a different glory than that revealed in John 12.

> "While you have the light, believe in the light, that you may become sons of the light." When Jesus had said these things, he departed and hid himself from them. Though he had done so many signs before them, they still did not believe in him, so that the word spoken by the prophet Isaiah might be fulfilled: "Lord, who has believed what he heard from us, and to whom has the arm of the Lord been revealed?" Therefore they could

*not believe. For again Isaiah said, "He has blinded their eyes
and hardened their heart, lest they see with their eyes, and
understand with their heart, and turn, and I would heal them."
Isaiah said these things because he saw his glory and spoke of
him. Nevertheless, many even of the authorities believed in him,
but for fear of the Pharisees they did not confess it, so that
they would not be put out of the synagogue; for they loved the
glory that comes from man more than the glory that comes
from God.*

—vv. 36-43

Until those who love the church, and especially those who lead
her as ministers of the Word, seek to restore the glory of Christ,
there will be no revival, no real reformation. This is the ultimate
goal of all ministry—the glory of the holy, sovereign Christ! Do
you realize that all claims to revival without the glory of Christ are
spurious? Why? Because Jesus clearly stated that the Spirit's work
will always be connected with His glory: "He will glorify me"
(John 16:14).

All modern efforts for reformation that center us in doctrine
as an end in itself will also accomplish nothing. I can't say this
too strongly. I fear modern attempts at reformation too easily miss
this crucial point. The radiance and splendor of Christ reflect the
Shekinah, the very glory of Yahweh. We do not recover this glory
by argumentation or by destroying the work of Christ in our
brothers and sisters (Col. 1:24-29) through personal attacks. We
need wisdom for sure. But we need divine wisdom, wisdom
revealed as the gift of God, the wisdom personified in Proverbs
that is to be found in the person of Christ alone. If you possess
Him, you have everything, and thus all wisdom. As the oft-quoted
saying goes:

All the armies that ever marched, and all the navies that ever were
built, and all the parliaments that ever sat, and all the kings that
ever reigned, put together, have not affected the life of mankind
on this earth as powerfully as has that one solitary life.[12]

Let me say this in a simple way that sets forth clearly what has been said.

> *Christ is glorious.*
> *Christ is very glorious.*
> *Christ is most glorious.*
> *Christ is always glorious.*
> *Christ is altogether glorious!*

We must labor to know this glory and to become mature in Christ. C. S. Lewis understood this when he wrote:

> God is no fonder of intellectual slackers than of any other slackers. If you are thinking of becoming a Christian, I warn you you are embarking on something which is going to take the whole of you, brains and all. But, fortunately, it works the other way round. Anyone who is honestly trying to be a Christian will soon find his intelligence being sharpened. One of the reasons why it needs no special education to be a Christian is that Christianity is an education itself. That is why an uneducated believer like Bunyan was able to write a book that has astonished the whole world.[13]

What we so desperately need today is to regain the glory of Christ. If we recover the sense of this glory, by the revelation of the Spirit to our souls, we shall arise to trust God as never before. And we will go forth with a power that is the power of God Almighty.

Several years ago N. T. Wright concluded an article titled "The New, Unimproved Jesus" with these words:

> We do not need to defend Jesus against attack, as the apostle Peter wrongly imagined as Jesus went toward the cross. We need instead to be grasped and transformed by the Jesus who was despised and rejected, belittled and battered. We need to discover afresh how to be for our world what he was for his; and that can only happen because we are committed to him as the center of history—God's loving and subversive presence at the very heart of his bruised and bleeding world.[14]

May the Lord hasten the day that we recover the glory of
Christ in the church of the West.

NOTES

1. *U. S News & World Report*, October 23, 2000.
2. John Calvin, *Psalms*, IV (Grand Rapids, MI: Baker, 1979), p. 358.
3. John Calvin, *Four Last Books of Moses*, I (Grand Rapids, MI: Baker, 1979), p. 423.
4. John Calvin, *Psalms*, IV, p. 291.
5. John Calvin, *Isaiah* IV, p. 424. (Grand Rapids, MI: Baker, 1979).
6. Francis Scott Key, "Lord, with Glowing Heart I'd Praise Thee."
7. N. T. Wright, *Tyndale New Testament Commentary: Colossians and Philemon* (Grand Rapids, MI: Eerdmans, 1986), pp. 70-71.
8. Peter T. O'Brien, *Word Biblical Commentary: Colossians and Philemon* (Waco, TX: Word, 1982), p. 61.
9. N. T. Wright, *Colossians and Philemon*, p. 74
10. Ibid., p. 75.
11. Charles H. Spurgeon, *The Metropolitan Tabernacle Pulpit*, "The Fulness of Christ, the Treasury of the Saints," 20:233-235.
12. Anonymous.
13. Edythe Draper, *Draper's Book of Quotations for the Christian World* (Wheaton, IL: Tyndale, 1992), p. 67.
14. N. T. Wright, "The New, Unimproved Jesus," *Christianity Today*, September 13, 1993.

2

THE GLORY OF THE
PERSON OF CHRIST

JAMES I. PACKER

THE LATE FRANCIS SCHAEFFER, surely one of the sharpest
Christian thinkers of the twentieth century, used to speak of *connotation words*. Both the modern world and the modern church,
to his mind, were full of them. What were they? *Connotation*
was once a standard term in the study of logic, where it stood for
a word's entire range of meaning, implication, and communicative
potency (what we would nowadays call its semantic field).
Connotations of words were nailed down by dictionary entries,
works of reference, and learned discussions in print, and thus they
became the criteria both of linguistically correct usage in communication and of what we would call politically correct reaction (attitudes and feelings of approval or disapproval, excitement
or coolness, admiration or contempt, and so on). What then did
Schaeffer mean by *connotation words*? He meant words that
had, so to speak, gone hollow through the eroding away of the
cognitive content they once carried—something that in intellectually shifting cultures inescapably happens—while yet they continue to evoke the emotions and attitudes that their original

content of meaning had called forth. Schaeffer wanted us to realize that this covert devaluing of words through erosion of their meaning really does happen, and that conventional people will become victims of the process through failure to see where it is taking place; and against that background he wanted to show us that the word *Christ* has become a case in point.

What did the word *Christ* originally signify? It is the Greek word *christos*, corresponding to the Hebrew *messiah*, meaning "the anointed one." In Jesus' day it was the title kept for God's long-promised Savior-King. From Pentecost morning on, Christian spokesmen applied the word to Jesus as His proper title of office and increasingly used it as if it were a personal proper name for the man from Nazareth "who was descended from David according to the flesh and was declared to be the Son of God in power according to the Spirit of holiness by his resurrection from the dead, Jesus Christ our Lord" (Rom. 1:3-4). Right from the start, historic Christianity has conceived the Christhood of Jesus in terms of His being the divine person whom the Father sent from heaven to become incarnate, to serve our race as prophet, priest, and king under conditions of humiliation, culminating in a redemptive death, then to rise, return to glory, and rule directly over the cosmos on His Father's behalf, imparting salvation to those for whom He won it, and thus creating and building up His church, until He reappears for resurrection, restoration, and retribution on judgment day. Through this doctrine, embodied as it is in all the church's liturgies and creeds and confessions and in countless hymns and praise songs, the word *Christ* has naturally become for Christians in the churches a source of feelings of awe and adoration as they compose their souls for communion with the Father and the Son through the Spirit, while for others it carries enough of a sense of supernatural sacred reality to make it an expressive swear word for use in times of shock. But while this goes on, so Schaeffer maintained, *Christ* has become a connotation word for many, for whom most, if not all, of the meaning that first called forth the feelings has drained away.

What Schaeffer had in view here was the drastically destructive effect that the desupernaturalizing acids of liberal theology have had on faith in the older Protestant church families. These acids (which dissolved away the truths of the Trinity; Jesus' personal divinity, virgin birth, miracles, bodily resurrection, and personal return; the atonement; and the entire economy of sovereign grace) were applied to the churches by theologians and pastors in the belief that altering the faith in this way would turn it into a new source of strength and influence in an increasingly secularized society. So they presented it as a spiritual advance, a refining of religion, and a salutary refocusing of Jesus as the model man, the archetypal Good Samaritan, the apostle and embodiment of God's boundless love, the supreme teacher of selfless service, and the fountainhead of inspiration for all who would raise the moral tone of society and generate greater goodwill in the world around us. The effect, however, was to lose the real Christ, the Christ of the New Testament and of almost two millennia of church life.

Wittingly or unwittingly, the liberals played a cultural confidence trick, trading on the feelings and attitudes of awe, reverence, and commitment that the word *Christ* continued to evoke while emptying it of the meaning that gave rise to those feelings and attitudes originally. As a result, liberal churches contain people who think of themselves as Christians following and revering Christ, but who have so lost touch with the truth about Him that He has really become an *x* to them, an unknown quantity, about whom they fantasize in a way that fudges the vital facts. Thus, they affirm that had Jesus not died on the cross, the world would never have known how deeply God loves us; but if asked whether Jesus died in our place, as a propitiatory sacrifice for our sins, they say no. They affirm that God was uniquely present in Jesus and revealed by Jesus; they hail Jesus as a man full of God in every way; but if asked whether Jesus was, and is, God the Son, the second person of the holy and undivided Three, they say no again. They may be passionate as worship leaders, ardent in exhorting to discipleship, totally committed to keeping the churches going, while yet, in Schaeffer's sense (and mine)—that is, in real biblical terms—they remain Christless. For them, at least, and unhappily, *Christ* has become a connotation word.

It needs to be said, before we go further, that at this point evangelicals, who are quick to pounce on liberal lapses from orthodoxy, often seem to have problems of their own. Their passion for confessional correctness easily induces a mind-set that shrinks knowledge of Jesus Christ from a precious, personal relationship of faith, hope, love, and adoration to a defensive verbal formula, sound but sterile, because the fellowship with Jesus to which the formula points, and into which it tells us to plunge, is not pursued. In my youth a lively Christian would be spoken of as one who "loves the Lord." I do not hear that phrase very often these days, and I sometimes wonder whether friendship with the Christ who loves us and calls us believers His friends bulks very large in our devotional lives. If asked to describe our relationship with the Lord Jesus, we all would probably say that we trust in His atoning blood, but I doubt whether many of us would be found saying, "He is my greatest Friend." Yet surely by the New Testament standard that is what we should all be saying. No doubt it is better to be biblically correct regarding Jesus Christ while falling short in devotion to Him and intimacy with Him than to be devoted to a Christ who is mostly a product of one's imagination and is therefore hardly real—but it is not much better. I hope that what I am about to say may help heal both sorts of shortcomings.

My declared theme is one facet of the glory of Jesus Christ— namely, the glory of His divine-human person. A comment on the word *glory* will set us going.

What is glory? In biblical usage, this word (Hebrew, *kabod*;

Greek, *doxa*) has two distinct but connected meanings. It signifies, first, divinity on display, God revealed in His praiseworthiness, and, second, grateful praise and adoration given to God both by word and by action for the praiseworthiness He has shown. The people of God are never in good spiritual health, never strong for spiritual witness and warfare, never energized through Christ in and for renewal until fellowship with God the Father and friendship with God the Son have become the mainspring of both individual and corporate life, and joy in praising God and giving Him glory has become a habit of the heart. We will now explore one of the supreme Bible presentations of the glory of Christ; may our journey take us all deeper into these realities.

The passage is the prologue to the fourth Gospel, John 1:1-18.

In the beginning was the Word, and the Word was with God, and the Word was God. He was in the beginning with God. All things were made through him, and without him was not anything made that was made. In him was life, and the life was the light of men. The light shines in the darkness, and the darkness has not overcome it.

There was a man sent from God, whose name was John. He came as a witness, to bear witness about the light, that all might believe through him. He was not the light, but came to bear witness about the light.

The true light, which enlightens everyone, was coming into the world. He was in the world, and the world was made through him, yet the world did not know him. He came to his own, and his own people did not receive him. But to all who did receive him, who believed in his name, he gave the right to become children of God, who were born, not of blood nor of the will of the flesh nor of the will of man, but of God.

And the Word became flesh and dwelt among us, and we have seen his glory, glory as of the only Son from the Father, full of grace and truth.

(John bore witness about him and cried out, "This was he of whom I said, 'He who comes after me ranks before me, because he was before me.'")

And from his fullness we have all received, grace upon grace. For the law was given through Moses; grace and truth came through Jesus Christ. No one has ever seen God; the only God, who is at the Father's side, he has made him known.

Central to this awesome passage is verse 14, with its three great assertions about the person we know as Jesus Christ (Jesus the Messiah, or Messiah Jesus, as some render the designation). The assertions are: (1) "The Word became flesh"—was incarnate, as we say, through taking to Himself everything involved in being human, as Adam was human; (2) the Word incarnate displayed in Himself, in His earthly ministry, the glory of His divine sonship; (3) the Word incarnate was "full of grace and truth," both of which He constantly exhibited and communicated. Verses 1-13 lead up to these assertions in a carefully planned way, as we shall see; verses 15-18 amplify the second and third of them; verse 17 gives us the human designation by which the incarnate Son of God is now known; and verse 18 shows the finality of the Son as both the revealer and the revelation of the Father. These tremendous assertions, couched as they are in such simple and straightforward language that their staggering, mind-blowing character is hardly felt at first, are the key John gives us to everything he goes on to narrate. He means his statements to have a depth-charge effect in readers' minds, and his calculated strategy to this end is the double take, whereby the real shockingness of what he says in the plain, economical Greek of which he is a master is discerned only on second thoughts—an unrivaled way of making an impact on the mind, if you can handle it properly, as John can. A review of how he has drafted the prologue shows all this very clearly.

Put yourself in John's shoes. Like the other three evangelists, he plans to write an account of Jesus' ministry—His preaching, teaching, disciplining, working wonders that were signs, finally His dying, rising, and continuing supernaturally at large—that would truly convey the Gospel, the good news of new life through Jesus, to all his readers, whoever they might be. He wants his book to take them into the full depth of his own understanding of Jesus and fellowship by faith with Jesus, as he himself says near the end, straight after recording Thomas's confession, "My Lord and my God!" (20:28): "These [significant doings of Jesus] are written so that you [readers] may believe that Jesus is the Christ, the Son of God, and that by believing you may have life in his name" (20:31). So how is he to start his story? With a prologue giving the clues to comprehending it—yes, that is his first decision, as we have seen. But how should the prologue start? If its opening words were, "In the beginning was the Son" or "the Son of God," Jewish readers, who knew these phrases as titles for Israel's king (see 2 Sam. 7:14; Ps. 2:6-12; etc.), would take John to be affirming the preexistence of a human Messiah, and Gentile readers, knowing Greek mythology, would think he was talking of a hero like Hercules, who had a divine father (Zeus, the top god) and a human mother. The thought John wanted to start with, of a second person within the divine being, would come across to neither of these readerships; rather, both would be wrongfooted intellectually from the word *go*. So a different way of starting had to be devised.

John's aim in the prologue was to introduce Jesus and establish the frame within which everything He said and did should be interpreted; also, to stir readers' interest, to engage their minds, and to show them what the book is going to be about. The strategy on which he settled to achieve these goals was brilliantly simple, and simply brilliant, as we see once we lay it out.

(1) He would first speak of the Logos (the Word) and present the thought of personal plurality within the divinity by saying that the Logos was with God in fellowship and was God in person.

This suited his plan perfectly, for Logos means essentially an idea, or line of thought, and John intended to display Jesus as expressing and embodying the Father's mind at every point. Also, both Jewish and Gentile thought leaders were speculating about a cosmic Logos about which they could not claim to know much, but which they thought of as somehow linking God with the world and fulfilling divine purposes and spreading divine wisdom within it. So John's opening sentence would lead them, not astray, but forward from where they were into deeper truth.

(2) He would then declare the cosmic functions of the Logos as the divine agent in creating everything ("through him," v. 3, expresses that), the source and sustainer of all forms of life that the universe contains ("in him," v. 4, expresses that), and as such the permanent and unfailing communicator of "light" to human beings. "Light" in all cultures and languages is an image of wisdom, insight, and understanding, and John would use this unspecific word to link up in readers' minds with whatever wisdom for rational living they thought they had already—their sense of God and of the good life, of eternity and ultimate reality, of right and wrong and final retribution, and so forth. Thus their hopeful expectation that John's book would help them understand the Logos better, taking their minds on from the place they were currently at, would be reinforced. An equally unspecific reference to "darkness" (see v. 5) trying and failing to put the light out would then alert readers to the fact that battles for truth against ignorance, error, unbelief, and misbelief have to be fought sooner or later in every heart; this would prepare them to face the questions of truth with which John's story of Jesus would confront them.

(3) John would then move to what Schaeffer called space-time history—the preparatory witness of John the Baptist (vv. 6-8), the personal presence as a human male of the Logos, the failure of His own (Jewish) people to recognize Him and their actual rejection of Him (vv. 9-11), and the giving of new, supernatural

birth and new life as children of God to all who did receive and put their trust in the Logos whom others spurned (vv. 12-13). Here John would bring in semi-technical terms ("believe," "receive," "born . . . of God," "children of God") that he would be using again as he told the full story of Jesus. He would not explain these words in the prologue (after all, a prologue is no more than an overture), but by introducing them he would prepare his readers' minds to process what was going to be presented to them—namely, the reality of new life from God through knowing and worshiping and following the Word made flesh. When aiming to explain a thing, it is always helpful to familiarize people with such standard terminology—technical language, that is—as is used for brevity and precision with regard to it, and John planned to do that here.

(4) By now, so John calculated, his readers would be asking, in effect: Who is this Word, the Logos who created, sustains, and enlightens everyone, who has actually lived in this world, and who, it seems, can impart a radically new and privileged life with God? Will you tell us, John, if you really know? And John would answer that question directly, in a very thorough way. He would state outright that the person in question is the Logos become human ("flesh" was the word that would express that), though without diminution of His divinity, as an explicit reference to His "glory" while here on earth would make plain. John would tell his readers that this divine-human visitor "dwelt"—using a simple picture-word that literally means "camped"—"among us"—the apostolic witnesses, with others—all of whom have since received "grace upon grace"—benefits in an endless flow—"from his fullness." John would give the divine visitor's human name and title—"Jesus Christ," Jesus the Messiah—and would announce that the witnesses discerned Him, through all the surface-level ordinariness in which His extraordinariness was anchored and earthed, to be in reality the divine Son of the divine Father, "full of grace and truth." The Logos, he would say, is the Son. Then

he would hammer home this identification in a startling way, by calling Jesus "the only God" (using a Greek adjective reserved for only sons) "who is at the Father's side," using the Greek phrase "in the Father's bosom," implying complete and unqualified intimacy; and he would round off with the thought that Jesus Christ is truly the unique revelation, demonstration, exhibition, and elucidation of God, who otherwise is essentially an enigma to us, and apart from the Word made flesh remains so. This climactic, categorical, black-and-white declaration would stand as a perspectival bridge to lead readers into an understanding of the story John would now unfold.

How can we tell that this was John's strategy when he wrote his prologue? Why, from the fact that this is exactly what he did. Thus, in just over 250 ordinary Greek words, using the Logos category as his bridge of communication, John established his key thought—namely, that Jesus is the divine Son. That this is his key thought is beyond doubt, for once he has stated it within the frame of divine plurality—that is, as we would say, in trinitarian terms—he drops the Logos category entirely. In the body of the Gospel we never meet it. It was only ever there as the linguistic equivalent of a flatbed truck, designed to carry the transcendent truth of Jesus' divine sonship to its proper destination in human hearts. Some second-, third-, and fourth-century writers spent their strength maintaining, mainly for apologetic purposes, that the personal Son should be thought of as the less-than-personal Logos; but that reverses the flow of John's thought, and if we are to grasp the glory of Christ's person in any adequate way, we must stay on John's wavelength. Jesus is the second person of the eternal Trinity, the holy Three who together are the one God who knows Himself, and would have us know Him, as the Father, the Son, and the Holy Spirit forever. As John's Gospel shows its readers in some detail, They are He, and He is They, and the person, place, and prerogatives of Jesus Christ cannot be understood in any other frame of reference.

Here, then, in the nutshell of John's prologue, the glory of Christ's person is set before us, and our task now is to apprehend and appreciate this as fully as we can. To this end, starting from the prologue, though not limiting myself to it, I state the four themes that follow.

INCARNATION MEANS MYSTERY

When Christian thinkers speak of mystery, they do not mean anything like a detective novel, in which the criminal is found out and all the puzzling evidence is explained before the end. Mystery in theology is a label, or classification, for all those divine realities that we confess as actual without knowing how they are possible. We know that they are, for the Bible tells us so, but it is beyond the reach of our creaturely minds to see how they can be. To say this is to offend human intellectual pride, and to admit it is very humbling, but that is what we have to do. Guided by Scripture, we can circumscribe divine mysteries in the sense of describing what they involve and result in, and differentiating them from other ideas about reality, and defending them against distortions and misrepresentations; but we cannot explain how God does them in such a sense that, given the power, we would know how to do them ourselves. Every aspect of God's triune life, and of His interacting with His creation, involves mystery, and we should not be surprised that the Incarnation is the supreme instance of this. When John says, "the Word became flesh," he not only locates a manifestation of the divine glory, but he also confronts us with a divine mystery. We know something of what happens in the womb when a pregnancy starts and as it develops, but when we try to imagine what was involved when the Holy Spirit overshadowed Mary and a divine-human fetus began to grow in her, we are out of our depth.

The way of wisdom is that when rational analysis can take us no further we turn to worship.

When reason fails, with all its powers,
Then faith prevails, and love adores.

So it should be with us all regarding the Incarnation. The
first facet of the glory of Christ's person is that through the wisdom, love, and power of God, He, the God-man, exists. The
Father's agent in creation has taken created human life into
Himself for all eternity. It sounds fantastic, but it is true. This is a
great and mighty wonder, a mystery in the full theological sense,
a reality that only God could cause to be. Endless praise is the only
fit response.

INCARNATION MEANS UNION

The union effected by the Incarnation or as, echoing John, we
might say, the enfleshing of the Son of God was of what the church
(not the Bible) has long called two natures, the divine and the
human, within the unity of a single personal life. As there was, and
is, a plurality of persons within the unity of God's essence, so there
was, and is, a conjunction of natures within Jesus Christ's person. To see what this means, think of a person as a self, a unit or
center of consciousness, memory, thought, imagination, emotions,
intentions, decisions, and relational responses, an "I" that knows
itself as "me" and engages with each other self as "you." And
think of a nature as a set of abilities and attitudes, of possibilities
for experiencing, of capacities for action and reaction. Personhood
has to do with who we are, with our identity and individuality and
distinctness from everyone else; nature has to do with what we
are, with our attitudes and habits, our strengths and limitations,
what gives us pleasure and what gives us pain, and the quality and
style of our living.

The effect of enfleshing was that in the Son's relationships to
both His father and people around, the perfections of humanity
and divinity come into view together. Jesus, as we see Him, is
one person, totally integrated (far more integrated, in fact, than

any of us are), a person who both as God and as man loves and obeys the Father and loves and serves other persons, and so is from every angle in both natures the true image of God. He acts always in the fullness of His two natures; the idea that from time to time one or the other was, so to speak, switched off, so that, for instance, He suffered "in His human nature (only)" or performed miracles "in His divine nature (only)" is a mistake, time-honored but nonetheless mistaken for that. It is a second facet of the glory of Christ's person that in Him the two natures were joined together "without confusion or change, indivisibly and inseparably," as the Council of Chalcedon in 451 put it, so that every excellence of both the divine and the human way of existing, behaving, and relating were seen in Him.

The mysteries of God as three persons in one essence and of Jesus Christ as one person in two natures are perhaps the two most difficult notions that the human mind has ever had to absorb, and it is no wonder that the early church struggled for centuries with both before a biblically exact way of verbalizing and circumscribing them was found. Regarding the Incarnation, the second doctrine of this foundational pair, the years before Chalcedon saw three troublesome blind alleys explored in disruptive ways. First, Apollinaris argued that the enfleshing was the taking of a human body without a human mind; then Nestorius was understood to maintain that it was the coming together of two persons, one divine and one human, to live under one skin so harmoniously as to look like one person only; and finally Eutyches contended that the humanity that the Son of God took to Himself in Mary's womb was so transmuted in the process that from His birth to His death and on beyond, Jesus the Savior was human no longer—having had two natures, He now had only one. Chalcedon's adverbs, cited above, were meant to rule out these ideas, and the good news is that they effectively did so, and do so still.

We cannot imagine what it felt like, on a moment-by-moment

basis, to have been Jesus the God-man on earth, but three biblical guidelines for thinking about His earthly life are as follows:

*It was never the way (that is, the nature) of the second person
of the Trinity to know, do, think, or say anything on His own
initiative, but only as His Father, the first person, led (John 5:19-
20).* But He was always told, and so always knew, with an imme-
diacy and a certainty that transcend our experience altogether,
what His Father's will for Him at each moment was (8:28-29;
12:49-50). His absolute submission to His Father meant, among
other things, that He only actualized His powers of omniscience
(the ability to have in His mind by an act of will immediate
knowledge of anything and everything—past, present, and
future) when, and so far as, His Father willed; hence, once or
twice He was ignorant of things He might have been expected
to know (e.g., 11:34; see also Mark 13:32; Luke 8:45-46). This
dependence on the Father, or subordination to the Father as some
would call it, is the one respect in which the Son, who is the
Father's full equal in nature (character, powers, attitudes) and
so fully reveals Him (John 14:8-11), is always less than the Father
(10:27-30; 14:28). This indeed is precisely why the first divine
person calls Himself, and is called, Father, while the second calls
Himself, and is called, Son. The Son's dependence on the Father's
leadership is an eternal fact, not a temporary condition that
enfleshing brought about; and to think otherwise seems to be
another time-honored mistake.

*The incarnate Lord lived through His body, as all of us
humans do, and so experienced firsthand the emotional and physical realities of weakness (hunger, thirst, tiredness, anxiety, pain
(see 4:6-7; 12:27; 13:21; 19:28), of anger at human evil (2:15-17),
and of grief at human distress (11:33-38).* Very rarely did the
Father lead Him to override the limits of embodied humanity
(6:19, the walking on water, is the only clear instance of such over-
riding in John's account of Jesus' pre-resurrection ministry). In
terms of life quality, the incarnate Son was truly one of us, and

to want to minimize this, supposing that reverence requires us to do so, is another hoary error from the past.

Being fully human, the incarnate Son could be, and was, tempted by the devil, the great manipulator of devices to bring the godly down. Like Adam, Jesus was tempted to disobey the Father, in all sorts of ways, some of which are clear from the gospel story as we have it. He was tempted to mishandle his messiahship, to indulge natural desires (for food, relaxation, friendship with the opposite sex, and so on) in a disorderly way, to express disappointment and distress at the spiritual sluggishness of His disciples and others in an unloving way, and so on. Unlike Adam, however, He fought off the devil every time. It was not in Him to sin—that is, it was His nature to resist temptation until He had overcome it. Divinity cannot sin; so incarnate divinity was certain to behave this way. But though He could not yield to temptation, He could not overcome it without a struggle, and one guesses that some of His struggles—that in Gethsemane, for instance—were more agonizing than any we have ever known. So to affirm that being divine He could not sin (which is true) does not in the least imply that victory over Satan's wiles came easily to Him (which would be false), and again it is misconceived reverence that fancies otherwise.

The Christ whom the four Gospels present to us with such consistent brilliance (the literary judgment is in place here; God chose outstanding writers) strikes the reader with almost unnerving force as a person who is both utterly different from everyone He rubbed shoulders with and yet who comes alongside them all with such insight, wisdom, and goodwill as only a stellar-quality human being could ever muster. Entirely one of us and yet not one of us at all—the formula sounds like a stupid contradiction, but in fact it reflects from the reader's standpoint the reality of the union of divine and human in this one person. This union of natures within the personhood of Christ is a further facet of His glory, as was said above, and to see, feel, affirm, won-

der at, and give praise and thanks for it, so far from constituting
stupidity, is simply to express God-given discernment in God-
honoring devotion.

INCARNATION MEANS ADDITION

Sympathy and empathy are not identical. Sympathy is your caring support of persons in distress, whether or not you have ever
known such distress yourself, while empathy means your caring
and supportive identification with others' experiences, bad or
good, which you knew so to speak from the inside, having, as we
say, been there yourself. Now, the effect of the Incarnation was
to add to the prior fact of divine sympathy with us in our struggles
a new fact—namely, divine empathy with us in literally the whole
of our lives.

My point is this: The Son of God lived a fully human life
before birth, through birth, infancy, childhood, and adolescence,
into adulthood. He experienced a wide cross section of human
relationships in the family and beyond. He knew what it was to
be taught and learn from Scripture, and daily to pray, and to
battle with the various forms of temptation that challenge wisdom and virtue. He entered into all the realities of love and hostility, of joy and disappointment, of popularity and unpopularity,
of pain, grief, and torture, agony of mind and body, and death.
Moreover (here is mystery again), His relation to our race was
such that every element of human experience became His in
principle, in an archetypal, generic, and inclusive way. In other
words, the experience of human life that He had enables Him to
enter empathetically into every bit of human experience as such.
Thus, He was not a woman, He never married, so far as we know
He was never sick or disabled, He never had to live with a
wasting disease or with the built-in temperamental flaws and
instabilities caused by manic-depressive, obsessive-compulsive,
schizophrenic, or phobic disorders, nor did He have to cope
with the physical and mental decline of old age. Yet by virtue of

His limited human experience He is able to enter fully and with no limitation at all into all of these human conditions, and to help us in all our attempts to grapple with them. "Because he himself has suffered when tempted, he is able to help those who are being tempted" (Heb. 2:18; see 4:15), whatever form their temptation may take.

Just as empathetic human help means more to us because of the empathy, so we should be stirred and spurred to look to Christ for divine help in our struggles by knowing of His empathy with us. Whenever we are being drawn into evil, folly, and despair in any form, we should tell ourselves that in a real sense Christ has been there before us and has overcome harder pressure than any we face; and now by His understanding presence He can keep us from falling and can enable us to reproduce His victory in our own lives. The writer to the Hebrews is emphatic on this (see 2:18; 4:14-16; 12:1-4). Christ's adding human empathy to divine sympathy, with its resultant richness of heavenly help, is part, at least, of the meaning of "full of grace" in John 1:14 and is one more facet of the glory of the person of our incarnate Lord.

A grotesque twisting of this theme is the so-called kenosis theory, which posits that in order to have a fully human experience, including limitation of strength and knowledge, the Son of God at the moment of enfleshing gave up the omniscience and omnipotence that were previously His, so that the addition to His divine life of human empathy was balanced by the subtracting from it of basic divine powers. Quite apart from its lack of scriptural support and the tritheistic quality of its idea that one person of the Godhead could thus reduce Himself to become less than the other two, the theory self-destructs by impaling itself on the horns of this dilemma: *either*, in order to stay fully human, the Son of God in heaven never recovers His lost powers, *or*, having recovered them, the Son of God in heaven has ceased to be fully human. Neither alternative is acceptable to biblical Christians; so the theory is doomed for all who think it through. Only muddleheadedness could imagine that kenotic fantasizing enhances the glory of the person of Christ.

INCARNATION MEANS MEDIATION

The supreme glory of the divine-human person of the incarnate Lord is that by it He was qualified to be the last Adam, the second representative head of the human race, and the substitutionary sin-bearer for sinful people like ourselves, who by His atoning death were reconciled to God; and thus He became the mediator whose ministry is the heart of the Gospel. "There is one God, and there is one mediator between God and men, the man Christ Jesus, who gave himself as a ransom for all, which is the testimony given at the proper time" (1 Tim. 2:5-6). For His ministry of achieving, attesting, and communicating redemption, the mediator needed to be both human and divine. As man for God, He must suffer an atoning death in our place as the climax of a life of flawless obedience; as God for man, He must declare the Gospel, first in His earthly ministry and then from His heavenly throne, and call on us to receive the reconciliation He has won for us by receiving Him through faith and repentance followed by a life of loyalty and love in devoted discipleship to Him. Without incarnation there would have been no God-man, and without the God-man there would have been no mediation, no revelation of redemption, because there would have been no redemption to reveal and no path to peace with God because the peacemaking on our behalf would not have been done. The enfleshing of the Son was thus integral to God's plan of salvation, and the glory of Christ's unique person must be seen as an aspect of the glory of the Gospel itself.

Space limits preclude any developing of this great theme here. Suffice it to say that whereas the idea, sometimes met, that the Incarnation would have taken place had there been no fall is pure speculation; the incarnating of the Son of God to become our divine-human Savior is basic to the entire New Testament. "God so loved the world, that he gave his only Son, that whoever believes in him should not perish but have eternal life" (John 3:16). In particular, the Incarnation is the key to understanding and benefiting from the four Gospels. When William Temple said that "Our reading of the gospel story can be and should be an act of personal communion with the living divine Lord," he was assuming not only the resurrection and heavenly reign of Christ, and the ministry of the Holy Spirit through the Scriptures, but also the Incarnation, without which no such communion as he envisages would ever have been possible. As it is, however, this fellowship with Christ, whereby again and again He steps out of the Gospels, as it were, into our lives, is simple Christian reality. I hope we all read the Gospels constantly and prove this in our own experience.

What then, specifically, should our study of the glory of Christ's person add up to for us in personal terms? Here I can do no better than stand aside and let John Newton, the old converted slave trader as he called himself, address that question in the simple, searching, homespun, didactic-devotional verse of which he was such a master. May I say, as I give place to him, that I am with him all the way in what he says, and I can wish nothing better for my readers than that they should be too.

> *What think ye of Christ? Is the test*
> *To try both your state and your scheme.*
> *You cannot be right in the rest*
> *Unless you think rightly of him.*
> *As Jesus appears in your view,*
> *As he is beloved or not,*
> *So God is disposed to you,*
> *And mercy or wrath is your lot.*
>
> *Some take him a creature to be,*
> *A man, or an angel at most;*
> *Sure these have not feelings like me,*
> *Nor know themselves wretched and lost;*

So guilty, so helpless am I,
I durst not confide in his blood,
Nor on his protection rely,
Unless I were sure he is God.

If asked what of Jesus I think,
Though still my best thoughts are but poor,
I say he's my meat and my drink,
My life and my strength and my store.
My Shepherd, my Husband, my Friend,
My Savior from sin and from thrall;
My hope from beginning to end,
My portion, my Lord, and my all.

3

THE GLORY OF CHRIST
AS MEDIATOR

R. ALBERT MOHLER, JR.

EVANGELICAL CHRISTIANS HAVE grown accustomed to the domestication of transcendence. This is a serious judgment upon us, and yet it is evident in our worship, our evangelism, and our lack of wonder. Moreover, we have lost the concept of glory. Indeed, it appears that the word *glory* is one of those words in the evangelical vocabulary that now passes us by without leaving any residue of meaning. It causes one to ponder what most evangelicals would do if worship depended upon a definition of the term.

Definition is a form of discipline; it is a responsibility of the stewardship of words. The biblical concept of *glory* is established in a specific linguistic history. In the Old Testament we discover that God's glory—God's *kabod*—is His own personal possession. In the New Testament we discover that God's glory—God's *doxa*—represents the fact that He is weighty. The Greeks recognized the necessity of a gentleman, a man among men, having *gravitas*. This is behind the understanding of weightiness that is ascribed to God.

Developing from the Bible's rich trajectory on this theme, it appears that God's glory ought to be understood *as the intrinsic reality and the external manifestation of God's greatness.* Those two dimensions are very important. For in Scripture there are references to God's glory increasing and decreasing. Such texts lead to this question: In God's solitude, in Himself, can He increase or decrease in glory?

The answer, of course, is absolutely not! God is infinite in all respects. Hence, in His intrinsic reality, His glory is absolutely infinite and eternal. What these texts do reveal, however, is that in its external manifestation, God's glory does wax and wane. Sometimes His glory is more evident than at others. Israel was reminded multifarious times that its responsibility was to declare the glory of God among the nations. That is now the church's responsibility. The church is called to be a people for God's glory. Notice, though, that it is a reflected glory; it does not intrinsically belong to the church. Rather, it is by virtue of Christ's atoning work that the church is enabled to reflect the glory of God.

Given the aforementioned state of affairs, however, there is a great need for rediscovery of God's glory. Make no mistake, *rediscovery* is precisely the right term, because that is what is required. The church stands in need, not merely of recovery, but of rediscovery. For this is not merely a case of an occasionally overlooked biblical theme. Rather, it is sadly the case that the evangelical church appears to have lost the knowledge of this theological category altogether.

In his *Institutes*, however, John Calvin has provided a nice remedy for this contagion from which the contemporary church could stand to benefit greatly. In book II, chapter 16, he records these words:

> We see our whole salvation and all its parts are comprehended in Christ [Acts 4:12]. We should therefore take care not to derive the least portion of it from anywhere else. If we seek salvation, we are taught by the very name of Jesus that it is "of him" [1 Cor. 1:30]. If we seek any other gifts of the Spirit,

they will be found in his anointing. If we seek strength, it lies in his dominion; if purity, in his conception; if gentleness, it appears in his birth. . . . If we seek redemption, it lies in his passion; if acquittal, in his condemnation; if remission of the curse, in his cross [Gal. 3:13]; if satisfaction, in his sacrifice; if purification, in his blood; if reconciliation, in his descent into hell; if mortification of the flesh, in his tomb; if newness of life, in his resurrection; if immortality, in the same; if inheritance of the Heavenly Kingdom, in his entrance into heaven; if protection, if security, if abundant supply of all blessings, in his kingdom; if untroubled expectation of judgment, in the power given him to judge. In short, since rich store of every kind of good abounds in him, let us drink our fill from this fountain, and from no other.[1]

May God, by His grace, be pleased to make that the pledge and determination of the church in the present day.

In considering Christ's glorious work as mediator, it is worth noting that, as a title, *Mediator* is intentionally comprehensive. It describes all the aspects of Christ's atoning work. Indeed, the title *Mediator* is quite possibly the most comprehensive of all the titles that apply to Christ's work.

To begin with, the title looks back to creation, where both Genesis 1 and John 1 converge to tell us that Jesus Christ was Himself the mediator of creation. "All things came into being through Him, and apart from Him nothing came into being that has come into being" (John 1:1).[2] The title *Mediator* obviously looks to Christ's priestly work of atonement on the cross. Beyond that, however, it also looks to our redemption and anticipates the consummation.

The wonder of Christ's comprehensive work was not lost on Paul, who expounded this point in Colossians 1:15-18 saying:

> *And He is the image of the invisible God, the firstborn of all creation. For by Him all things were created, both in the heavens and on earth, visible and invisible, whether thrones or dominions or rulers or authorities—all things have been created*

*through Him and for Him. He is before all things, and in Him
all things hold together. He is also head of the body, the church;
and He is the beginning, the firstborn from the dead, so that He
Himself will come to have first place in everything.*

In considering the glory of Christ and His work, it is of
utmost importance to acknowledge that His preeminence is
absolutely central. An understanding of salvation should not first
prompt reference to the self, but to Christ who saves.
Undoubtedly, for the Christian who would pursue an increasingly
God-centered worldview, any contemplation of Christ and His
work must necessarily be concerned to display His preeminence,
to the increase of His glory.

Unfortunately, however, there are confusions about Christ's
work as mediator. There are those who think of a mediator as a
negotiator in a labor dispute. When two parties are at an impasse,
an external agent is brought in who has no commitment to either
side but has expertise in trying to establish common ground and
negotiate some kind of concord or contract between two oppos-
ing parties that will bring about a common ground.

Suffice it to say that any such depiction of Christ's mediatorial work is altogether inadequate. For Christ has not come as a
neutral third party, and He certainly does not enter as an agent
with dispassionate objectivity about the parties that are in con-
tention. In fact, the parties never even get to a table except by
His mediatorial work. As the Bible makes clear, mankind is not
merely disaffected from God but is an enemy of God. Indeed, God
in His holiness cannot tolerate sin, and in the jealous preservation of His holiness to His own glory, there can be no common
ground; there can be no negotiated settlement.

Jesus Christ is mediator by God's grace and by the Father's initiative. According to the Bible, Christ is mediator because God
sovereignly determined to save sinners by the means of the mediatorial work of His Son. Moreover, any discussion of Christ as

mediator necessarily evokes reference to his three offices—prophet, priest, and king. As prophet, Christ is the revealer of true knowledge; as priest, He is the remover of the guilt of sin; and as king, He is ruler over all.

Consider, as the central text in the remaining discussion, Hebrews 9:11-15. The author of the letter to the Hebrews writes:

> *But when Christ appeared as a high priest of the good things to come, He entered through the greater and more perfect tabernacle, not made with hands, that is to say, not of this creation; and not through the blood of goats and calves, but through His own blood, He entered the holy place once for all, having obtained eternal redemption. For if the blood of goats and bulls and the ashes of a heifer sprinkling those who have been defiled sanctify for the cleansing of the flesh, how much more will the blood of Christ, who through the eternal Spirit offered Himself without blemish to God, cleanse your conscience from dead works to serve the living God? For this reason He is the mediator of a new covenant, so that, since a death has taken place for the redemption of the transgressions that were committed under the first covenant, those who have been called may receive the promise of the eternal inheritance.*

"The promise of the eternal inheritance." It is clear, in this text, that Jesus Christ is the mediator of a new covenant. This means, first of all, that this new covenant is superior to the first covenant. That much is confirmed in 10:1, where Christ is acknowledged as a high priest of the good things to come. What had the prophets of old foretold? There would be good things to come, better than the first covenant. In short, there is no way to preach Christ without proclaiming Him as the mediator of a new covenant. He is the high priest of the good things to come. He brought those good things; He is those good things; He accomplished those good things.

This text teaches that Christ has entered the greater and "more perfect tabernacle," a tabernacle not made with human hands. This word "tabernacle" refers to a "tent of meeting." It is noteworthy to recall that it was not the Israelites' idea to establish the tabernacle; rather, it was God's design and order.

Recall Exodus 40:34-38, where it is told how the tent of meeting was visited by God:

> Then the cloud covered the tent of meeting, and the glory of the LORD filled the tabernacle. Moses was not able to enter the tent of meeting because the cloud had settled on it, and the glory of the LORD filled the tabernacle. Throughout all their journeys whenever the cloud was taken up from over the tabernacle, the sons of Israel would set out; but if the cloud was not taken up, then they did not set out until the day when it was taken up. For throughout their journeys, the cloud of the LORD was on the tabernacle by day, and there was fire in it by night, in the sight of all the house of Israel.

One has to understand that passage in order to understand John 1:14 where we learn that "the Word became flesh, and dwelt among us, and we saw His glory, glory as of the only begotten from the Father, full of grace and truth." On this side of the cross, what was formerly seen in a tabernacle, a column of fire and a column of smoke, is now seen in all its fullness in the glory of Christ. He entered the greater and more perfect tabernacle, not one made with human hands.

Hebrews 9:24 makes this clear: "For Christ did not enter a holy place made with hands, a mere copy of the true one, but into heaven itself, now to appear in the presence of God for us." This helps clarify what took place in the Holy of Holies, which was the Old Testament epicenter of the manifestation of God's glory, as in heaven. But glorious though it was, it was nevertheless a shadow, "a mere copy." When the high priest went in with the blood of an innocent animal on the Day of Atonement, and when the blood was sprinkled on the mercy seat, it pointed to Christ.

Yet Christ, in accomplishing atonement as our great high

priest, did not enter a tabernacle made with human hands. He is not a human high priest who must offer the sacrifice over and over, and He is not a human high priest whose work, by God's order, will atone only for the external sins. Christ's work reaches the inner man, as is made clear in this text. Moreover, He entered into a greater tabernacle, which is defined in the text as heaven itself, and it is there that His intercessory work is done. For this reason, as the book of Hebrews explains, Christ is the mediator of a new covenant.

Christ's own words recorded in Luke 22:20 confirm this: "And in the same way He took the cup after they had eaten, saying, 'This cup which is poured out for you is the new covenant in My blood.'" This is the language of Christ's priestly work. It is indeed the case then, as Hebrews makes clear, that Jesus is the great high priest. His work accomplished, once for all, our salvation, and it gave us the promise of the eternal inheritance—an inheritance that cannot be taken away.

Let us now examine the mediatorial work of Christ in several of its dimensions. First, consider Christ, *the suffering mediator*. Recall Hebrews 9:12: "[A]nd not through the blood of goats and calves, but through His own blood, He entered the holy place once for all." As evidenced here, suffering is central to the understanding of the mediatorial work of Christ. Think back for a moment to the Old Testament where, in the sacrificial system, there was certainly suffering experienced by the animal whose life was poured out. In those cases the suffering was involuntary. Moreover, it was not a salvific suffering. Christ, however, experienced and fulfilled the suffering that is central to the cross.

As Mark 8:31 indicates, Jesus Himself noted and anticipated this reality during His earthly ministry: "And He began to teach them that the Son of Man must suffer many things and be rejected by the elders and the chief priests and the scribes, and be killed, and after three days rise again." Clearly here Christ is referring back to Isaiah's prophecy of the suffering servant, and looking at the Isaiah passage serves as a poignant reminder that we must learn to see the glory of God manifested in the sufferings of Christ.

According to Isaiah 53:3-5, which prophetically anticipated Christ's mediatorial work:

> *He was despised and forsaken of men, a man of sorrows and acquainted with grief; and like one from whom men hide their face He was despised, and we did not esteem Him. Surely our griefs He Himself bore, and our sorrows He carried; yet we ourselves esteemed Him stricken, smitten of God, and afflicted. But He was pierced through for our transgressions, He was crushed for our iniquities; the chastening for our well-being fell upon Him, and by His scourging we are healed.*

Isaac Watts understood that the glory of God is manifest in Christ's sufferings, an understanding reflected in his wonderful hymn about the atoning work of Christ, "When I Survey the Wondrous Cross."

> *See from his head, his hands, his feet,*
> *Sorrow and love flow mingled down!*
> *Did e'er such love and sorrow meet,*
> *Or thorns compose so rich a crown!*[3]

Upon looking at the sufferings of Christ, one discovers not the defeat, deflection, or disaster of one whose ministry plans were interrupted by the cross. Rather, one discovers the Lamb of God slain before the foundation of the world. There is seen the one who came to die, and He is seen to fulfill His mediatorial work, with all of its glory, on that cross. And so we see the glory of Christ, our suffering mediator.

Second, Christ is rightly understood to be *the sacrificial mediator*. "For this reason He is the mediator of a new covenant, so that, since a death has taken place for the redemption of the transgressions that were committed under the first covenant, those who have been called may receive the promise of the eternal inheritance" (Heb. 9:15). That Christ is our sacrificial mediator has perhaps been encapsulated most powerfully by John Owen, and this he did in the very title of his greatest work, *The Death of Death in the Death of Christ*.[4] Death died in Christ's death. The end of death was seen in the cross of Christ. Believers see Christ's glory in the fact that He was their sacrifice—indeed, a sacrifice unlike any previous sacrifice.

The writer of Hebrews demonstrates this repetitively. On the Day of Atonement the high priest of old offered the blood of an innocent animal—according to verse 12, "the blood of goats and calves," according to verse 13, "a heifer." Christ, however, offered His own blood. When He entered that greater and more perfect tabernacle, He did not take in the blood of an innocent animal. Instead, He took in the blood of the innocent Lamb of God. At the very turning point of history, God the Son shed His own blood for the remission of our sins.

Consequently, when believers declare the Gospel, they declare Christ's glory as mediator, for He is the substitute for sinners. John Stott has noted that in this respect the blood speaks to three very important aspects of redemption. First, "blood is the symbol of life."[5] According to Deuteronomy 12:23, "the blood is the life." Second, "blood makes atonement."[6] That is consistent throughout the Old Testament. And third, "blood was given by God for this atoning purpose."[7] The Lord Himself demanded that blood should be the means of the remission of sins. Leviticus 17:11 reads, "For the life of the flesh is in the blood, and I have given it to you on the altar to make atonement for your souls; for it is the blood by reason of the life that makes atonement."

But the blood that was shed in the Holy of Holies—in the tabernacle made with human hands—did not ultimately give eternal life. It did not, itself, lead to the eternal inheritance. These sacrifices were not an administration of the New Covenant; rather, they presented a shadow of things to come. As the book of

Hebrews declares, those shadows were fulfilled in Christ our high priest, our suffering mediator, our sacrificial mediator. In Christ the work was completed, and the blood was shed; not the blood of a lamb, but of the Lamb of God. And so God's glory is displayed in Christ's glory as our sacrificial mediator.

Third, Christ is *the saving mediator*. His glory is manifest in His saving work. According to Hebrews 9:12, He "obtained eternal redemption." That is, He saved sinners from the due penalty of their sins.

Some would complain here that evangelicals sound like a broken record, repeating the refrain of salvation and redemption over and over. To which, of course, the proper response is, "What other message do we have? This is the Gospel, and in it we see Christ's glory." Christ is the saving mediator. This is simply the Gospel. He obtained eternal redemption. His work of salvation is the central theme of Scripture—anticipated and prepared for in the Old Testament, fulfilled and focused in the New. Throughout the pages of the Bible we see the saving work of Christ as high priest.

The title *Savior*, which conveys a function of Christ's mediatorial work, declares His glory. The angels declared it to the shepherds in Luke 2:11, "for today in the city of David there has been born for you a Savior, who is Christ the Lord." In Peter's defense before the counsel in Acts 5:30-31 he said, "The God of our fathers raised up Jesus, whom you had put to death by hanging Him on a cross. He is the one whom God exalted to His right hand as a Prince and a Savior, to grant repentance to Israel, and forgiveness of sins." Jesus is our Savior, and we see Christ's glory preeminently in His saving work.

Christ is also *our substitutionary mediator*. In June 2000, the Southern Baptist Convention adopted a revised form of our Confession of Faith, *The Baptist Faith and Message*. By God's grace something remarkable happened—namely, a major American denomination revised its confession of faith, not in creeping toward liberalism, but in embracing more evangelical and biblical convictions.

One of the corrections involved inserting the word *justification* in several critical places. Another key revision involved clearly defining Christ's atonement as a substitutionary work. This revision was necessary as substitution is being increasingly denied in quarters where the Gospel offends modern sensibilities. Some would have us believe that the substitutionary understanding of the atonement is simply one theory among others.

Unfortunately for these proponents, the apostle Paul did not see it that way. Substitution is central to the proclamation of the cross. Other theories of the atonement may add something to our understanding of the substitutionary nature of Christ's work, but His work can never be anything less than fully and comprehensively substitutionary. "Penal substitution" is not merely a Latin theory of the atonement; it is, in fact, what the apostles preached.

Needless to say, this revision of *The Baptist Faith and Message* led to some controversy in our denomination. Some were disaffected, and on leaving us they charged, "There you have it; there's the agenda. They have finally shown that they are going to go back and try to demand that substitution is the understanding of the atonement."

The truth of the matter is that we have no right to demand it, but Scripture does. It is not our determination. Rather, it is the declaration of God's own Word. But in evangelicalism today there is an opposition—indeed, an allergic reaction—to the notion of Christ's substitutionary work.

Apart from Christ's penal substitutionary atonement, there is no "good news" for sinners. Yet I have had a theologian directly say to me, "I don't want any more of this bloody cross religion." What is abundantly clear from the Scriptures, however, is that there is no Christianity without it.

Feminist theologians say that the substitutionary understanding of the atonement portrays a form of divine child abuse, and they refuse to have any of it for the sake of the subjugated victim. In the "Reimagining God" conference, notorious for 1993, Virginia Mollenkott said, "I can no longer worship in a theological context that depicts God as an abusive parent and Jesus as the obedient trusting child. This violent theology encourages the violence of our streets and our nations."[8]

Delores Williams, who evidently thought Mollenkott was too tepid, put it bluntly, saying, "I don't think we need a theory of atonement at all. Atonement has to do so much with death. I don't think we need folks hanging on crosses and blood dripping and weird stuff."[9] Evidently that is the theological manifesto of Williams and others.

In spite of the fact that some may call it "weird stuff," the church must confess that this is not something we invented. On the contrary, this is God's sovereign wisdom, His sovereign determination. It confounds the wisdom of the wise; it is foolishness to Greeks and a stumbling block to Jews; indeed, it is the Gospel, and there is no other gospel.

Sadly, however, this is being compromised, even among evangelicals. In the book *Unbounded Love* by Clark Pinnock and Robert Brow the authors tell us, "We have to overcome the rational theory of atonement, based on Latin judicial categories, that has dominated Western theology. It demotes the resurrection from its central place and changes the cross from scandal to abstract theory. It makes things sound as if God *wanted* Jesus to die and predestined Pilate and Caiaphas to make it happen. Surely not— Jesus is God's beloved Son."[10]

They complain that in the preaching of the cross—in the preaching of Christ as the willing penal substitute—it is made to appear that God intended this all along. Once again, however, the church did not make this up. Remember the words of Peter before the Sanhedrin: "For truly in this city there were gathered together against Your holy servant Jesus, whom You anointed, both Herod and Pontius Pilate, along with the Gentiles and the peoples of Israel, to do whatever Your hand and Your purpose predestined to occur" (Acts 4:27-28).

Apparently, though, these theologians believe that as God observed the incarnate Son, He must have been thinking to Himself, *It's going to be interesting to see how this turns out.* Brow and Pinnock further argue:

> We must realize that Jesus did not die in order to change God's attitude towards us but to change our attitude to God. God, who took the initiative of reconciling the world, does not need reconciling. It is in us that the decisive change is needed. The cross was not a sacrifice without which God could not love or forgive us; it was a sacrifice without which we would not have been able to accept forgiveness. The problem lies with us, not with God. He requires no sacrifice except a broken and contrite heart.[11]

Recall, however, that Paul said, "God was in Christ reconciling the world to Himself" (2 Cor. 5:19). The cross took place not just to show us God's love, but to atone for sin. Sin demanded atonement, and Christ, the Mediator, provided that atonement.

But once again, Brow and Pinnock would have us believe:

> By experiencing suffering as a human being by reason of incarnation, God gained a moral authority and credibility in regard to overcoming evil in humans which he did not have before. In bearing our sorrows and becoming acquainted with our grief, God became a fellow sufferer and learned to understand us. A suffering God has moral credibility for dealing with our sin. The cross changed God, but not in the way we have thought. It did not change his attitude toward sinners from wrath to love. It did add to the divine experience, however, and qualified God to reconcile and transform sinners. God in Jesus died to sin and came to life to make salvation possible through union with him.[12]

Such a statement is nothing other than a denial of the cross of Christ. God did not go to the cross in order to learn something. The cross is not about God gaining the moral credibility needed to identify with our suffering. Rather, we are transformed by the penal substitutionary work of Christ so that all who believe in Him might not perish but have everlasting life. Hebrews 9:22 reminds us that under the Old Covenant there was no forgiveness without the shedding of blood. But Christ, our great high priest, took not the blood of a calf or a goat but shed His own blood for the remission of our sins.

Martyn Lloyd-Jones told the story of hearing two men having a dispute about the Gospel. The nonbeliever said of the recently converted man, "Of course, I have great respect for my friend here, he is a good man; I can see what has happened to him: that is all right, and he does a lot of good and I agree with that; but you know," he said, "what I can't stand is this blood and thunder business that he keeps on talking about."[13] Lloyd-Jones then reflected, "The blood of Christ! People have referred to it as 'this butchery,' 'this wallowing in blood.' By all means let us live a good life, they say, let us worship God, but must you drag in this blood perpetually? It seems a scandal to them, it seems something hateful."[14]

This "blood and thunder" element was the cause of the trouble. Yet even today men make this same judgment. There are many who object to this as primitive religion, finding it grotesque and offensive to refined sensibilities. Lloyd-Jones was keen in his observation. The hatred of the cross does not come because people misunderstand it. The most intense hatred comes when they do understand it but do not come to it by faith.

The apostle Paul made abundantly clear that the substitutionary understanding of Christ's work is central. In 1 Corinthians 15:1-5 he wrote:

> Now I make known to you, brethren, the gospel which I
> preached to you, which also you received, in which also you
> stand, by which also you are saved, if you hold fast the word
> which I preached to you, unless you believed in vain. For I

> delivered to you as of first importance what I also received, that
> Christ died for our sins according to the Scriptures, and that He
> was buried, and that He was raised on the third day according
> to the Scriptures, and that He appeared to Cephas, then to the
> twelve.

Paul said it was "of first importance . . . that Christ died for
our sins according to the Scriptures." We glory in the cross, and
we are right to do so, because on the cross Christ is displayed in
all His glory as our mediator and as our substitute—the high priest
who was Himself the sacrifice.

Next we understand Christ as *the superior mediator*. The
writer of Hebrews identified Christ as the mediator of a new
covenant, a covenant that is superior to the first. The first
covenant did not save. Indeed, it could not save. Hebrews 8:6
reads, "But now He has obtained a more excellent ministry, by
as much as He is also the mediator of a better covenant, which has
been enacted on better promises."

This text makes clear that the provisions of the Old Covenant
merely provided an external washing of the taint of sin. It did
not transform the heart of stone into a living heart. Nor did it
make the Jews new men and women in Christ. That reality had
to await the passing away of the shadows and the appearing on
the cross of the accomplished work of Christ. He is the mediator
of a new covenant, and this is a superior covenant.

Hebrews 8—9 clearly display this. Christ has "obtained a
more excellent ministry." The old things, the shadows, have
passed away, and now we behold the glory of the Savior, the mediator of a new covenant.

Next, we see that Christ is *the supernatural mediator*. The
New Testament makes it abundantly clear that the mediator
who accomplished our salvation was fully God and fully man.
Hebrews 7 explains why this was necessary. The human high
priest had to repeat the Day of Atonement sacrifice in the Holy
of Holies year after year. But not only did the sacrifice have to be

repeated, it affected the external only, not the internal—the temporal, not the eternal. Christ, however, as the mediator of the superior covenant, provided a sin atonement that was not merely external but internal, not only temporal but eternal. Indeed, His was an atonement for sin once for all. It never can be, will be, or need be repeated. Jesus the Christ is our intercessor forever.

Hebrews 4:14-16 speaks clearly of Christ's humanity:

> *Therefore, since we have a great high priest who has passed through the heavens, Jesus the Son of God, let us hold fast our confession. For we do not have a high priest who cannot sympathize with our weaknesses, but One who has been tempted in all things as we are, yet without sin. Therefore let us draw near with confidence to the throne of grace, so that we may receive mercy and find grace to help in time of need.*

When Jesus Christ, on the cross, atoned for our sins, and when, in heaven, He entered the Holy of Holies, He offered not the blood of an innocent animal, but the blood of the innocent Lamb of God. As our mediator, He was fully God and fully man. He bore our griefs. He received our stripes. Indeed, He experienced temptation in every way as do we, yet without sin.

Both His humanity and deity are absolutely essential to His mediatorial work. We glory in the supernatural mediator who is both God and man in the Incarnation and in His atoning work. We glory in His deity and in His humanity, and both in absolutely full measure. The truth of the Gospel hangs there in the balance. It is central to Christ's mediatorial work.

Next we see that Christ was *the solitary mediator*. Paul writing in 1 Timothy 2:5-6 said, "For there is one God, and one mediator also between God and men, the man Christ Jesus, who gave Himself as a ransom for all, the testimony given at the proper time."

Scripture does not teach that Christ was *a* mediator. He is *the* Mediator, the one mediator. There are not many; there are not several—there is only one. This speaks of the absolute centrality and exclusivity of the saving work of Christ. We understand from Christ's own words that this is not negotiable for orthodox evangelical Christianity; it is the Gospel. "I am the way, and the truth, and the life; no one comes to the Father but through Me" (John 14:6). He alone purchased our salvation, and salvation comes alone to those who trust in Him. He is our solitary mediator, and in Him we see God's glory.

Christ was also *the sufficient mediator*. Hebrews 10 makes very clear that Christ's work is a completed work. There is nothing that remains to be done. It is fully accomplished. "It is finished," said the Lord, and it was.

Hebrews 10:18 put it thus: "Now where there is forgiveness of these things, there is no longer any offering for sin." This is why the bloody Mass is an abhorrence, because Christ is not sacrificed repeatedly. His sacrifice was once for all. We declare it and we preach it as an accomplished act and a sufficient atonement. We glory in Christ, the sufficient mediator. Nothing can be added to His work, and nothing can be taken from it.

Last, Christ is *our sovereign mediator*. He is not only prophet, He is not only priest, He is king. He rules over all. This element is missing in so much evangelical worship, where Christ is not seen, in the present, as the reigning king. He is indeed, however, the King of kings and Lord of lords, and He is so even today (cf. Heb. 1:5-13).

Let us take a page from the book of the Reformation. For the Reformation was about the Gospel. Martin Luther was not plunged into his deep and frightful depressions because he was concerned with some kind of theological nicety. He was concerned with how he would ever be found righteous, for he knew himself to be a sinner. By God's grace he discovered justification by faith—on which the church stands or falls—and he came to understand that salvation was not about anything he could do, but what

Christ had already done. And when he understood that "the just
shall live by his faith," he could say:

> There I began to understand that the righteousness of God is
> that by which the righteous lives by a gift of God, namely by
> faith. And this is the meaning: the righteousness of God is
> revealed by the gospel, namely, the passive righteousness with
> which merciful God justifies us by faith. . . . Here I felt that I
> was altogether born again and had entered paradise itself
> through open gates. There a totally other face of the entire
> Scripture showed itself to me.[15]

When we see Christ's glory, we look into the Holy of Holies,
and there, according to Romans 3, we see Christ as our propitiation. Focus on Christ our mercy seat, where His blood was shed
for the remission of our sins. Thus the Father receives all those
who are in Christ in such a way that He remains both "just and
the justifier of the one who has faith in Jesus" (Rom. 3:26).

That is the glory of the cross. That is the glory of the mediatorial work of Christ. It is the glory that will see us to glory.
And our only proper response is to glory in Jesus Christ our
mediator.

NOTES

1. John Calvin, *Institutes of the Christian Religion*, 2.16.19, ed. John T. McNeill, trans.
   Ford Lewis Battles, Library of Christian Classics, Vols. 20-21 (Philadelphia:
   Westminster, 1960), pp. 527-528.
2. Quoted from the *New American Standard Bible*. Unless otherwise noted, all biblical
   citations in this chapter will be taken from the NASB.
3. *The Psalms and Hymns of Isaac Watts* (Morgan, PA: Soli Deo Gloria, 1997), p. 526.
4. John Owen, *The Death of Death in the Death of Christ*, in *The Works of John Owen*,
   ed. William H. Goold, Vol. 10 (London: Johnstone & Hunter, 1852; repr. Edinburgh
   and Carlisle, PA: Banner of Truth Trust, 1967), pp. 140-428.
5. John R. W. Stott, *The Cross of Christ* (Downers Grove, IL: InterVarsity Press, 1986),
   p. 138.
6. Ibid.
7. Ibid.
8. Susan Cyre, "Mainline Denial: How Our churches Are Responding to 'Re-Imagining,'"
   Good News 27/5 (1994), pp. 12-13.
9. Dottie Chase, "United Methodist Women Get Taste of Sophia Worship," *Good News*
   27/4 (1994), pp. 36-38. It is perhaps interesting to note that Williams has tenure at
   Union Theological Seminary in New York.

10. Clark H. Pinnock and Robert C. Brow, *Unbounded Love: A Good News Theology for the 21st Century* (Downers Grove, IL: InterVarsity Press, 1994), p. 102.

11. Ibid., p. 103.

12. Ibid., pp. 105-106.

13. D. Martyn Lloyd-Jones, *God's Way of Reconciliation: Studies in Ephesians Chapter 2* (Grand Rapids, MI: Baker, 1972), pp. 191-192.

14. Ibid., p. 192.

15. Martin Luther, *Preface to the Complete Edition of Luther's Latin Writings*, in *Luther's Works*, eds. Jaroslav Pelikan (Vols. 1-30) and Helmut T. Lehmann (Vols. 31-55), Vol. 34, *Career of the Reformer: IV*, ed. Lewis W. Spitz, trans. Lewis W. Spitz (Philadelphia: Fortress Press, 1960), p. 337.

4

THE GLORY OF
THE LAMB

JIM ELLIFF

I HAVE ALWAYS BEEN attracted to the word *apogee*. The literal meaning is, "away from the earth," from the Latin, *apogaeum* or the Greek *apogaion*. In Ptolemaic astronomy, when the earth was thought to be at the center of the universe, the sun was said to be at its apogee on the longest day of the year. In common usage, the word now means the highest point, the climax, or the culmination of something.

Revelation 4—5 sets before us the apogee of the theology of the cross. I am using the word *cross* here as a theological idea, inclusive of not only the historical redemptive act, but also the entire galaxy of implications spinning out from that one act. We come to the climactic scene in these chapters.

The prospect of the cross traverses the shadow-lands of the Old Testament, to the reality in the Gospels, and on to redemption's vivifying power in the Acts and the epistles. But in Revelation we see the most dazzling depiction of all, as the heavenly court glories in the Lamb slain, and the inhabitants of heaven sing loudly about the power and glory of the cross. One is taken aback by the emphasis on the cross in the Revelation. Heaven does not "get over" the cross, as if there are better things to think about.

On earth some of our more knowing brethren have said, or at least thought, "I've gotten the idea of the cross clearly in my thinking; so now I can ponder things of much greater theological importance." But then they pass away, with some massive tome about a little known theological vagary on their chest, and are ushered into heaven only to find that the angels and created beings, as well as the Father Himself, are obsessed with the very subject they left behind years ago. Heaven is not only Christocentric, it is cruci-centric, and quite blaring about it.

We will begin with chapter 4, but my aim is to eventually get to the new song in 5:9, where we will see brilliantly displayed the glory of the Lamb and His powerful redemption. Attempt to see and relish the beauty of this scene as you step now into the worship session of heaven.

John writes:

> *After this I looked, and behold, a door standing open in heaven! And the first voice, which I had heard speaking to me like a trumpet, said, "Come up here, and I will show you what must take place after this."*
>
> *At once I was in the Spirit, and behold, a throne stood in heaven, with one seated on the throne. And he who sat there had the appearance of jasper and carnelian, and around the throne was a rainbow that had the appearance of an emerald. Around the throne were twenty-four thrones, and seated on the thrones were twenty-four elders, clothed in white garments, with golden crowns on their heads.*
>
> *From the throne came flashes of lightning, and rumblings and peals of thunder, and before the throne were burning seven torches of fire, which are the seven spirits of God, and before the throne there was as it were a sea of glass, like crystal. And around the throne, on each side of the throne, are four living creatures, full of eyes in front and behind: the first living creature like a lion, the second living creature like an ox, the third*

living creature with the face of a man, and the fourth living
creature like an eagle in flight.

And the four living creatures, each of them with six wings,
are full of eyes all around and within, and day or night they
never cease to say, "Holy, holy, holy, is the Lord God Almighty,
who was and is and is to come!" And whenever the living crea-
tures give glory and honor and thanks to him who is seated
on the throne, who lives forever and ever, the twenty-four elders
fall down before him who is seated on the throne and worship
him who lives forever and ever. They cast their crowns before
the throne, saying, "Worthy are you, our Lord and God, to
receive glory and honor and power, for you created all things,
and by your will they existed and were created."

—4:1-11

The living creatures around the throne are constantly saying, "Holy, holy, holy." It is as if they look at the Lord, gasp, and exclaim, "Holy, holy, holy." They look again, take another gasp, and exclaim, "Holy, holy, holy." They cannot quit saying, "Holy, holy, holy."

Then there is the repeated action by the twenty-four elders, who fall down and cast their crowns before Him. Perhaps this means that each elder removes his crown when he falls before Him and places it before Him as a symbol. The text says that "whenever" the living creatures give glory, the elders cast down their crowns, and so it appears to be a repeated ceremony. Over and over they cast their crowns before the Lord, giving evidence to the fact that everything is owed to Him, everything comes from the Lord, and He is the creator of all things.

In chapter 5 we come to a place at which, if this were a sheet of music, there would be a crescendo mark. Those of you who do not know much about music must have noticed on a musical score some little *f*'s written here and there. That *f* stands for *forte*, an Italian word meaning strong or loud. An *ff* stands for the superlative of *forte* or *fortissimo*, and *fff* or *ffff* stands for the superlative of *fortissimo* and is called *fortemente*. We come to a

fortemente in this chapter. I want you to feel the crescendo leading up to the new song that is going to be sung before the Lord.
Now look at what happens—the action is building dramatically.

> *Then I saw in the right hand of him who was seated on the*
> *throne a scroll written within and on the back, sealed with*
> *seven seals. And I saw a strong angel proclaiming with a loud*
> *voice, "Who is worthy to open the scroll and break its seals?"*
> *And no one in heaven or on earth or under the earth was*
> *able to open the scroll or to look into it, and I began to weep*
> *loudly because no one was found worthy to open the scroll or*
> *to look into it. And one of the elders said to me, "Weep no*
> *more; behold, the Lion of the tribe of Judah, the Root of David,*
> *has conquered, so that he can open the scroll and its seven*
> *seals."*
> *And between the throne and the four living creatures and*
> *among the elders I saw a Lamb standing, as though it had*
> *been slain, with seven horns and seven eyes, which are the seven*
> *spirits of God sent out into all the earth. And he went out and*
> *took the scroll from the right hand of him who was seated on*
> *the throne.*
>
> —5:1-7

Can you feel the crescendo? You would expect, after the elder
speaks of the Lion and the Root of David, that John would then
see some vision such as the one we find in the first chapter of the
book of the Revelation—a *powerful* kind of manifestation.

But what do we find? We find something quite strange and
arresting—the manifestation of the Lamb, the Lamb as if slain,
with seven horns and seven eyes. It is an unusual picture, is it not?
The seven horns speak of strength. The seven eyes speak of the
Spirit of God. This pictures the kind of relationship that the Trinity
has, with the Son emanating from the Father, the Spirit emanating
from the Son, all three coexisting, and all three the same in essence.
You get a sense of that relationship in Revelation 5.

And so this all-knowing and all-powerful or *prevailing*
Lamb—the One who has conquered the power of sin and death—

is the One who takes the scroll of the judgments of God that are about to unfold in the book of the Revelation. The Bible says in John 5 that Jesus is given authority to execute judgment because He is the Son of man. He became incarnate. He came and added humanity to His deity, becoming the God-man. In that form He overcame the power of sin and death. So He is justly the One who should rule over what He overcame. He is the One who can open the scrolls of the judgments of God, which explode throughout the rest of the book of the Revelation.

Now we come to the *fortemente* of the passage.

> *And when he had taken the scroll, the four living creatures and the twenty-four elders fell down before the Lamb, each holding a harp, and golden bowls full of incense, which are the prayers of the saints. And they sang a new song, saying, "Worthy are you to take the scroll and to open its seals, for you were slain, and by your blood you ransomed people for God from every tribe and language and people and nation, and you have made them a kingdom and priests to our God, and they shall reign on the earth."*
>
> —5:8-10

These songs, or praise choruses, are replete throughout the book of the Revelation. But why is this song called a *new* song?

Let me give a bit of conjecture here about this song and why it is called *new*. I believe that this revelation in heaven of the second person of the Godhead as the Lamb slain was a shocking revelation. In this image there is a representation of a type of mercy about which heaven's created beings knew nothing. They know something about the *judgment* of God, especially in light of a certain number of angels who fell. There was no mercy for those who fell. And there was no mercy toward elect angels either, because they had no sin. In a strange way, mercy was absent.

Jesus now demonstrates Himself preeminently as the Lamb who has acted mercifully toward certain people, and this is such a different and new thing that even angels long to look into it.

Mercy is an important concept, but often misunderstood. Biblically there are two types of mercy. There is what we might call a pure mercy, which is being described here. There is also a temporary mercy that God bestows upon the unjust. A temporary mercy for the unjust, though it is a true mercy, is in fact an eternal agony. An unjust person sins against the temporary mercy that he has been given. If the rain falls on the unjust, and God is merciful toward him, and that individual continues in his resistance against God, he is in fact making his judgment that much worse. That is what Romans 2 describes for us. Paul says that these merciful things God does ought to lead men to repentance, but because of their stubborn hearts they are storing up wrath for themselves in the day of wrath, when everything will finally be revealed.

Here John is speaking of what I call a *pure* mercy because it is mediated to us through the cross. Since God is just, He obviously cannot *justly* pour mercy upon you apart from the death of Jesus Christ. I know that the cross justifies you before God, but here I am talking about how God justifies His behavior toward you.

Healing would be an example of a merciful act. People sometimes ask the question, "Is healing part of the atonement?" I know what they mean. They want to be able to say that they may claim healing for anyone at any time. The truth is, God *sovereignly* dispenses healing. But I will say this: Every mercy that God gives to the elect is only justified by the atonement. This and this alone is the kind of mercy that will not kick back on you and cause you agony in the future. This mercy, then, demands a *new* song. The mediated mercies of God are what cause us to have confidence that "for those who love God all things work together for good, for those who are called according to his purpose" (Rom. 8:28).

In Revelation 5 the creatures before the Lord erupt into this beautiful song as a way of exalting the glory of the Lamb that is seen through His powerful redemption. Why is this such a powerful and glorious redemption? Look at the text again.

> *And they sang a new song, saying, "Worthy are you to take the scroll and to open its seals, for you were slain, and by your blood you ransomed people for God from every tribe and language and people and nation, and have made us a kingdom and priests to God, and they shall reign on the earth."*
>
> —vv. 9-10

This is a powerful and glorious thing, first, because His redemption did *completely* what He intended it to do. Not the mountains of man's sins, nor the raging fury and craftiness of Satan and his demons, nor the grip of death itself could thwart Christ from accomplishing His purpose. He is said to have accomplished something, and what He accomplished was the purchasing of certain individuals out of all of the tribes and nations and peoples of the world.

He redeemed or ransomed or purchased men for God. Note the tense of the verb—it is *done*, it is *complete*. Some would say, "Jesus' sufferings on the cross made all men redeemable." This is not what is said here. John reports that the elders and creatures declared that *everything* necessary for us to be purchased from the slavery of sin has been done by Jesus Christ, and nothing more needs to be added to that work. He has purchased us completely. He has bought us and redeemed us fully. This is not a *potentiality*—it is an *actuality*.

The divine order is like this: God elects you from eternity past, He sends His Son as redeemer to purchase you for Himself, then He sends His Holy Spirit to those He has redeemed to apply that redemption to their lives.

Do you see why I say that? It is very important to understand it this way. He has redeemed you, though later the Holy Spirit will come and apply that redemption by drawing you to conviction and instructing you in the Gospel and working in you to

believe. He will apply that which has happened on the cross. It is
redemption, as John Murray referred to it, "accomplished and
applied."

There is real beauty in that statement. Many years ago I heard
Eric Alexander, the well-known Scottish minister, address this
issue. Though I saw myself as a man understanding many tenets
of Reformed Christianity, I was struggling with the issue of how
far the atonement went and for whom it was actually accomplished. Was it for *all* men, or was it for those *certain* people who
are called the elect of God?

When I heard Eric Alexander preach on 2 Corinthians 5 I
turned to someone and said, very simply, "He died for *me*." At
that moment I broke out in profuse weeping. I realized the impact
of the fact that when Jesus Christ died, He literally had my name
in His mind. He actually knew the one for whom He was dying.
Out of all the tribes and tongues and peoples, there I was, there
was Jim Elliff. Jesus Christ went to the cross with me on His heart,
and with you on His heart if you are one of His.

The logical construct of the Puritan theologian John Owen
certainly applies here, and some of you know it well. But for those
of you who may not, let me repeat it for you in my own words.

> If Christ died for all men and paid for the sins of all men,
> including their sin of unbelief, then all men will go to heaven,
> and you must be a universalist.

> If Christ died for all men, and paid fully for the sins of all
> men, except their sin of unbelief, then every man must surely be
> damned to hell, for every man has lived in unbelief.

So the only logical way to look at this, according to Owen, is
to see that Jesus Christ died for *all* of the sins of *some* people,
including their sin of unbelief. If you believe this, you are believing correctly. Christ actually substituted Himself for those He chose
to save. To say that Christ substituted for some who will experience

none of its effect removes all meaning from the lovely word *sub-stitutionary* as in the phrase "substitutionary atonement."

This *finished* aspect of the cross is what this passage in Revelation teaches so forcefully, perhaps better than any other passage. It is exegetically correct as well as theologically sound to say that Jesus Christ accomplished a complete work. If you look carefully at words such as *redemption, reconciliation,* and *propitiation,* you will find that Scripture repeatedly presents these as *completed* actions, something *fully* done, and never to be done again. All that was necessary to purchase you from sin has already been done by Jesus Christ.

Suppose you eat in a restaurant this afternoon. Further suppose that you will sit at a table with some friends, and I will sit at another table with some other friends. Suppose you get up, go to the counter, and pay for my lunch. If the cashier is honest, he will not charge me again when I try to pay for my own meal. It has been paid for in full. It has been done. I may not believe it, yet it has been truly done. God certainly is honest, is He not? There can be no double jeopardy with God toward the damned that would say to them, "Your sins are covered" and then require payment for those sins at the judgment (Rev. 20:11-15).

If all the sins of all people have been paid for, why does the Bible say that some will stand before a judgment, in which God condemns them and assigns to them punishment related to those very sins, including every idle word and secret thought? If those sins have been paid for, they have been paid for. An honest God would not punish sinners for what has already been paid. He charges some because Jesus did not pay for their sin. But the elect have been redeemed fully.

Have you grasped the beauty of this? All the toxic waste of your life has been dumped on Jesus Christ, and He has *really* made propitiation for you (1 John 4:10).

Charles Spurgeon, the great nineteenth-century preacher, put it this way:

Let the Christian feel that the teaching which lowers the work
of Christ, makes it dependent upon the will of man as to its
effect, puts the cross on the ground and saith "That blood is
shed, but it may be shed in vain, shed in vain for you,"—let us
all feel that such teaching cometh not from the Spirit of God.
That teaching it is, which pointing to the cross saith, "He shall
see the travail of the soul, and shall be satisfied;" that teaching
which makes the atonement a true atonement which puts away
the vindictive justice of God forever from every soul for whom
that atonement was offered, exalts Christ, and, therefore, it is
a teaching which comes from the Spirit of God. When your
heart is brought to rest upon what Christ has done, when lay-
ing aside all confidence in your own works, knowledge, pray-
ings, doings, or believings, you come to rest upon what Christ
has done in its simplicity, then is Jesus Christ exalted in your
heart, and it must have been the work of the Spirit of divine
grace. The person then, and the work of Christ are exalted.[1]

We should also note that this redemption is powerful and
glorious precisely because this complete work was done so *extensively*. The passage says that people have been redeemed or purchased for God by His blood out of *every tribe and tongue and
people and nation*. His mercy is as broad as the ocean.

This expansiveness is so even though Satan exercises an
authority over this present world. Revelation 13:7 says concerning the Antichrist: "It was allowed to make war on the saints
and to conquer them. And authority was given it over every tribe
and people and language and nation." So here we have saints
actually being overcome, martyred, killed, and put to the test
by the enemy of our souls. Authority over all the tribes and the
nations and the tongues of people is given to that foe. "The
whole world," the Bible says, "lies in the power of the evil one"
(1 John 5:19). But it is out of that terrible, disgusting rulership
in this world in the atmospheric realm that Christ has done this
extensive work of redeeming people from every tribe and nation.
The Bible is emphasizing just how powerful this redemption
really is.

In Acts 1:8 the resurrected Christ says to His disciples, "And you will be my witnesses in Jerusalem and in all Judea and Samaria, and to the end of the earth." Is that a command? No; it is really *not* a command if you look at it carefully. What is it then? It is a prophetic declaration! Luke 24 says the same thing. Repentance and remission of sins *will be preached* to the whole world. As we read that prophetic declaration and then come to the end of the New Testament, we see that in fact it is so. People from every tribe, nation, and tongue—wherever this Word is preached—will be represented in heaven. God says it will be preached everywhere with solid effect.

So when we send out missionaries from our churches, we find that their job is not one that is pathetic. They should never feel overcome. Nor should they quote statistics in order to inform us that things are miserable, because they are not so miserable in terms of God's plan. God is exactly on schedule, and He's not one soul behind.

The missionaries that we send go in the outflow of this prophetic declaration. They go out as witnesses, actually picking up the spoils of Christ's redemption. Thus God is allowing us a co-participation with Him in this great enterprise that He will most assuredly accomplish, right to the last soul. What a glorious unfolding we see between the declaration of Acts 1:8 and the reality in Revelation 5:9. And we get to be part of it all!

So it is a powerful thing that Jesus Christ did in redeeming us so completely and so extensively. We can tell our friends who wonder about the graciousness of our Lord, "Look, every tribe will be represented in heaven—*every tribe.* That is how much God spreads His love throughout this world!"

We should also note that this redemption is powerful and glorious because this completed work, which extends to include millions of people, was done so *lavishly.* Look at the passage in Revelation again: "And by your blood," it says, "you ransomed people for God from every tribe and language and people and nation, and *you have made them a kingdom and priests to our God, and they shall reign on the earth.*"

When my wife's grandmother died, the family became the heir of all that she had. This included *everything*—all that was beautiful or memorable, but also the food in the refrigerator, the Chihuahua, and even the trash in the trash can. As believers we also inherit everything with Christ, and we will rule over everything with Him. We will judge the angels and this world as we take our place in heaven's hierarchy. We are subordinate regents with Christ! Think about this: We were slaves who were to be pitied, embarrassingly controlled by sin and damned for it, but now we are made kings! There is a complete change of status, and this change was accomplished through a powerful redemption.

Israel was called a kingdom of priests because it had some priests among it, representing the people, but we have been given an exalted status beyond this. *All* of us are priests, the Scripture says, and we stand with the high priest in the privileged position of being on the other side of the veil. There is something spectacular about this truth. The one who *could* not and *would* not talk with God now has this as his eternal job assignment and privilege. You have become a priest to the Lord, and you shall reign.

I am not going to reveal an eschatology that I do not know I have, but the Scripture clearly says, "They shall reign on the earth." I will let you work out what that means with your own scheme of things, but I will tell you this: You will reign. There is an already/not yet aspect to this for sure. You already reign, right now, in heavenly places over all principalities and powers. You are not ultimately controlled by them. You reign above them. You are an overcomer in that sense. But there will be the future fulfillment of all this as well.

There is a stone relief that you may have seen if you have ever been a student of Roman culture. The relief is on the inner curve of the arch of Titus in the ancient Roman forum. It is often portrayed in books. It depicts the return of Titus from the Jewish wars. They are carrying back spoils of the victory with much excitement. There you see the golden altar, the trumpets, and the seven-branched oil lamp that obviously came from the temple compound. You can almost hear the shouts. You can sense the pawing and the snorting of the horses in this vivid relief. The crowd is cheering.

If you look carefully at this relief in the arch of Titus, you will see a long procession of people. These people are the slaves, the Jewish slaves who are to be sold on the auction blocks of Rome. If you look even more carefully, I think you will see yourself. Not as a Jewish slave obviously, but you certainly were a slave to your sin, a tyrant worse than Titus. You who once were such a slave, not innocently because you were caught up in a war and were captured, but a slave to sin by your own will, have been lavishly redeemed by Christ, and now you stand as a king and a priest. Imagine that!

And now, I wish to add one final *forte*, a *forte fortemente*, so to speak. Let's read the last four verses.

> *Then I looked, and I heard around the throne and the living creatures and the elders the voice of many angels, numbering myriads of myriads and thousands of thousands, saying with a loud voice, "Worthy is the Lamb who was slain, to receive power and wealth and wisdom and might and honor and glory and blessing!" And I heard every creature in heaven and on earth and under the earth and in the sea, and all that are in them, saying, "To him who sits on the throne and to the Lamb be blessing and honor and glory and might forever and ever!" And the four living creatures said, "Amen!" and the twenty-four elders fell down and worshiped.*
>
> —5:11-14

When we are prone to think of the cross in a diminutive way, forgetting its grandeur, its accomplishment, its power, then remember what the angels think of it all and what we will see and sing at a future date when things are clearer.

You could not manufacture such a scheme, such a monumental plan as God has worked out through this glorious Lamb. You are there in the intent of it all! It is you and I who should sing with great feeling and excitement and *fortemente,* "Crown him with many crowns, the Lamb upon his throne!"

NOTES

1. "The Spirit's Office Toward Disciples," a sermon preached April 23, 1865, *The C. H. Spurgeon Collection* (Ages Digital Library, 1998).

5

THE GLORY OF
CHRIST CRUCIFIED

JOHN H. ARMSTRONG

CYRIL (C. 310-386), fourth-century bishop of the church in Jerusalem, was one of the greatest early church defenders of the Nicene doctrine regarding the person of Christ. Perhaps his most famous contribution was the *Catechetical Lectures*. He wrote these for those who desired to join the church. In these lectures Cyril focused upon the importance of Jesus' death, burial, and resurrection as the cornerstone of true Christian faith. He plainly shows that he understood something of the glory of Christ crucified.

> If any disbelieve the power of the Crucified, let him ask the devils; if any believe not words, let him believe what he sees. Many have been crucified throughout the world, but by none of these are the devils scared; but when they see even the Sign of the Cross of Christ, who was crucified for us, they shudder.[1]

Cyril further added, "All kings when they die have their property extinguished with their life: but Christ crucified is worshipped by the whole world. We proclaim the crucified."[2] When we speak

of the glory of Christ, nowhere is that glory more evident than in
His crucifixion and death. Yet most Christians seem to live and die
without seeing much of the resplendent mystery of this cruciform glory.

The apostle Paul, reflecting on his own ministry, said, "We
preach Christ crucified" (1 Cor. 1:23). Yes, Paul would surely have
agreed with Cyril. The message is Christ crucified! This truth sums
up the apostolic message, the apostolic purpose, indeed the apostolic understanding of power!

Paul faced many false charges during his lifetime. Perhaps
none was more damaging than when he was charged with
ministerial duplicity. This amounted to an accusation that he
was, at the end of the day, a religious hypocrite. This charge is
precisely the one he faced in Galatia. If the charge ever caught
on, effective ministry would have been, for all intents and purposes, over.

But why was Paul charged in this way? The letter to the
Galatians tells us that he had been accused of preaching "circumcision." This seems quite foreign to us, but it was crucial in
the context of Paul's life and ministry. His critics were apparently
suggesting that he was *inconsistent*. The particular spin placed
upon Paul's ministry by those whom he refers to as the enemies
of the cross was potentially destructive. We are entitled to wonder,
where did this charge originate?

The trail takes us first to Acts 16, where we read of Paul having Timothy circumcised.

> *Paul came also to Derbe and to Lystra. A disciple was there,*
> *named Timothy, the son of a Jewish woman who was a believer,*
> *but his father was a Greek. He was well spoken of by the broth-*
> *ers at Lystra and Iconium. Paul wanted Timothy to accompany*
> *him, and he took him and circumcised him because of the Jews*
> *who were in those places, for they all knew that his father was*
> *a Greek.*
>
> —vv. 1-3

Then in 1 Corinthians 9 we read the following autobiographical comment:

> *For though I am free from all, I have made myself a servant to all, that I might win more of them. To the Jews I became as a Jew, in order to win Jews. To those under the law I became as one under the law (though not being myself under the law) that I might win those under the law.*
>
> —vv. 19-20

It isn't really astounding that critics found grounds to attack Paul when you consider his indifference to circumcision expressed earlier in this same epistle:

> *Was anyone at the time of his call already circumcised? Let him not seek to remove the marks of circumcision. Was anyone at the time of his call uncircumcised? Let him not seek circumcision. For neither circumcision counts for anything nor uncircumcision, but keeping the commandments of God.*
>
> —7:18-19

Whatever the situation in Galatia, Paul's detractors had clearly accused him, as I said earlier, of ministerial double-mindedness. He countered this charge with a simple question: "Why [if I preach circumcision] am I still being persecuted?" (Gal. 5:11). In other words, if the Judaizers in Galatia were still attacking Paul, and they were, then how do you explain his present persecution if he was practicing the very rite they held to be so important? Paul reasoned something like this: "If I were still preaching circumcision, they would simply leave me alone. But they haven't left me alone; so I am *not* doing what they charge me with doing." But what I want to draw particularly from Paul's argument comes later in verse 11. Here is the great theology behind this argument. We call this the theology of the cross. The idea comes in the last words of the verse: "In that case [if I were preaching circumcision as they charge] the offense of the cross has been removed."

THE OFFENSE OF THE CROSS?

Curtis Vaughn makes the very plausible suggestion that circumcision held the exact same place in the theology of the Judaizers that the cross did in Paul's theology, thus underscoring that Paul's theology was self-consciously rooted in the cross.[3] Thus, the *real offense* to these false teachers in Galatia was the cross of Christ, not the presence or absence of circumcision as a rite to be preserved. But why? The great early church preacher John Chrysostom (345-407) believed that "the cross was such a stumbling block because it led them [various Jews] to a failure to require obedience to the ancestral laws of the Jews."

Don't miss the point here. For Paul the entirety of his Christian faith and experience is based upon the central truth of the crucifixion and the resultant sacrificial death of Jesus. This can be seen in a number of passages in the New Testament, but none quite so clearly as Paul's amazing personal appeal in 1 Corinthians 1.

> For the word of the cross is folly to those who are perishing, but to us who are being saved it is the power of God. For it is written, "I will destroy the wisdom of the wise, and the discernment of the discerning I will thwart." Where is the one who is wise? Where is the scribe? Where is the debater of this age? Has not God made foolish the wisdom of the world? For since, in the wisdom of God, the world did not know God through wisdom, it pleased God through the folly of what we preach to save those who believe. For Jews demand signs and Greeks seek wisdom, but we preach Christ crucified, a stumbling block to Jews and folly to Gentiles, but to those who are called, both Jews and Greeks, Christ the power of God and the wisdom of God. For the foolishness of God is wiser than men, and the weakness of God is stronger than men.
>
> —vv. 18-25

The same theme runs like a thread through the whole letter to the Galatians. Consider the following:

We ourselves are Jews by birth and not Gentile sinners; yet we know that a person is not justified by works of the law but through faith in Jesus Christ, so we also have believed in Christ Jesus, in order to be justified by faith in Christ and not by works of the law, because by works of the law no one will be justified.

—2:15-16

And then consider this further development:

O foolish Galatians! Who has bewitched you? It was before your eyes that Jesus Christ was publicly portrayed as crucified. Let me ask you only this: Did you receive the Spirit by the works of the law or by hearing with faith?

—3:1-2

Finally, note what Paul says in the last chapter of Galatians:

It is those who want to make a good showing in the flesh who would force you to be circumcised, and only in order that they may not be persecuted for the cross of Christ. For even those who are circumcised do not themselves keep the law, but they desire to have you circumcised that they may boast in your flesh. But far be it from me to boast except in the cross of our Lord Jesus Christ, by which the world has been crucified to me, and I to the world.

—6:12-14

Paul calls the cross an "offense" in Galations 5:11. The Greek word translated "offense" is the ancient word *skandalon*. In the New Testament, when this term is used as a noun it refers to an "obstacle" in one's path (cf. Rom. 14:13; 16:17). When it is used as a verb, as in 1 Corinthians 8:13, it refers to that which will "make my brother stumble."

In his important work on Galatians, the contemporary scholar Hans Deiter Betz observes that "a *skandalon* refers to something which turns out to be a trap, a source of embarrassment and offense, a provocation which arouses resentment and resistance."[4] When you read the word *offense* in your English Bible, think of these synonyms: a trap, a source of embarrassment, or a provocation that brings resistance and resentment. You then will begin to get some idea of how the theology of the cross struck ordinary people in the first century.

Paul uses a type of shorthand by employing one very rich and strong word, *skandalon*. By this one word he sets forward that which is the central glory of *the entire message of the Gospel*, the good news—the cross of Christ! To speak of the cross of Christ is to speak, in the simplest way, of the Gospel of God's grace. The glory of the Gospel is revealed preeminently here, in the cross. Here is the mystery of all divine mysteries. The cross, a horrible gibbet designed by the Romans who took great delight in death and suffering, becomes the glorious symbol and power of Christian salvation.

This message of the cross was, and remains, an offense. To the Romans the cross was a particular symbol of defeat. The proud Roman patrician thus looked upon Jesus as defeated. He considered with utter contempt any person who died as a commoner on a cross. Jesus, to the Romans, was a loser. To win was the great goal, and Jesus of Nazareth lost! To the Hebrews the cross was a place of complete disgrace. Did not the Old Covenant plainly say that "Anyone hung on a tree is under God's curse" (Deut. 21:23, NIV)? How could one cut off from God in such shame save anyone? How could this be the Jewish Messiah? How could this be a revelation of the divine glory in any sense of the word?

HOW THE SCANDAL BECOMES GLORY

On the last evening that Jesus spent with His disciples, before the cross, John records that:

> When he [Judas] had gone out, Jesus said, "Now is the Son of Man glorified, and God is glorified in him. If God is glorified in him, God will also glorify him in himself, and glorify him at once."
>
> —JOHN 13:31-32

J. C. Ryle, in his oft succinct and poignant notes on the Gospels, writes:

> There is a dark and mysterious saying here and we may well believe that the eleven did not understand it. And no wonder! In all the agony of the death on the cross, in all the ignominy and humiliation which they saw afar off, or heard of the next day, in hanging naked for six hours between two thieves—in all this there was no appearance of glory! On the contrary, it was an event calculated to fill the minds of the Apostles with shame, disappointment, and dismay. And yet our Lord's saying was true.[5]

But what does the Gospel writer mean by the word "glorified" in John 13? This is, in reality, one of the greatest themes of the fourth Gospel. Examples of its use abound. All these references seem particularly connected to the event of the cross as the great historic moment when the glory of Christ was revealed to those who believed the mystery of the Gospel. The Gospel was revealed, to put it plainly, in the cruciform shape of the God-man who died there for sinners. In the previous chapter of John's Gospel we read, "The hour has come for the Son of Man to be glorified" (12:23). And then later we read, "But for this purpose I have come to this hour. Father, glorify your name" (12:27-28). But how, we must ask, is Christ *glorified in the cross*?

How wonderful to have heard of this glory at His baptism. How great was the glory at His transfiguration. But the cross—how can that reveal His glory? Yet this is what the inspired writer says. Here, at Calvary, He is most glorified in His person and in His work. Let me elaborate by providing several reasons why this is so.

1. He is glorified in the cross in that here *He performed the greatest work the whole of history has ever seen or ever will see*. Think of it. Here one man does for the race what no other man could or will do. Here one fully human man dies for a multitude and thus opens the life gate to the entire race. Here the

perfectly innocent one lays down His life for His enemies, not just for His friends.

2. But we must also note that at the cross *Jesus reversed the conduct of the first Adam and thus turned the human race around in one redemptive act.* The first man plunged himself and all his posterity into hopelessness and death. The second man, Christ, rescues and redeems. The whole creation is deeply altered by this one act (Rom. 8:18-25).

3. Furthermore, *the death of Jesus destroyed the one who had the power of death.*

> *Since therefore the children share in flesh and blood, he himself likewise partook of the same things, that through death he might destroy the one who has the power of death, that is, the devil, and deliver all those who through fear of death were subject to lifelong slavery.*
>
> —HEB. 2:14-15

4. *Jesus paid, in His death, the ransom price for a people.* By this act He brings people from every tribe, nation, and tongue to glory.

> *For it was fitting that he, for whom and by whom all things exist, in bringing many sons to glory, should make the founder of their salvation perfect through suffering. For he who sanctifies and those who are sanctified all have one origin.*
>
> —HEB. 2:10-11A

5. Finally, *the manner of these sufferings also glorified Him.* The prophet glimpsed this hundreds of years beforehand.

> *He was oppressed, and he was afflicted, yet he opened not his mouth; like a lamb that is led to the slaughter, and like a sheep that before its shearers is silent, so he opened not his mouth. By oppression and judgment he was taken away; and as for his generation, who considered that he was cut off out of the land of the living, stricken for the transgression of my people? . . . Yet it was the will of the Lord to crush him; he*

has put him to grief; when his soul makes an offering for sin,
he shall see his offspring; he shall prolong his days; the will
of the LORD *shall prosper in his hand. Out of the anguish of*
his soul he shall see and be satisfied; by his knowledge shall the
righteous one, my servant, make many to be accounted right-
eous, and he shall bear their iniquities.

—ISA. 53:7-8, 10-11

Jesus willingly suffered. He was led, not driven, to the slaugh-
ter. As a result of His voluntary sacrifice He is now at the Father's
right hand—a glorified Savior who accomplished *all* that His
Father gave Him to do.

In the prayer of Jesus in John 17 the Savior prayed with this
glory in full view.

"The glory that you have given me I have given them, that
they may be one, even as we are one, I in them and you in me,
that they may become perfectly one, so that the world may
know that you sent me and loved them even as you loved me."

—VV. 22-23

But this death is glory in another remarkable sense. John
13:31-32 says that "God is glorified in him." In the context this
means the Father too is glorified in the death of Christ. What a
magnificent theme this glory really is! One cannot do justice to
it. William Hendriksen tries when he writes:

Due to the infinite closeness existing between the Sender and
the One sent (cf. [John] 10:30), God was glorified in him. The
two are inseparable. Whenever we think of Christ's sufferings,
we never know what to admire most: whether it be voluntary
self-surrender of the Son to such a death for such people, or
the willingness of the Father to give up such a Son to such a
death for such a people.[6]

Now think for a moment about *how* the Father is actually
glorified in the death of the Son. There are several ways that
bear consideration.

1. The *justice* of God the Father is exceedingly glorified in the cross of Christ. Exodus 34:7 says, "[The Lord God] will by no means clear the guilty." And in Romans the apostle says that God (the Father) gave Christ (the Son) over to death on the cross "to show his righteousness at the present time, so that he might be just and the justifier of the one who has faith in Jesus" (3:26). Think of it. The cross magnifies God's justice and righteousness. If God were not holy, righteous, and just, the cross was not necessary at all. In the biblical sense this is truly an exceedingly great glory.

2. The *power* of God is also openly glorified at the cross. Christ is crucified in weakness, and yet this weakness was the very strength of God on public display. This is why Paul says, "For the foolishness of God is wiser than men, and the weakness of God is stronger than men" (1 Cor. 1:25). Indeed, as Jesus Himself said, God's "power is made perfect in weakness" (2 Cor. 12:9). This is one of the amazing truths revealed by the theology of glory in the cross.

3. The *holiness* of God is uniquely glorified in the cross. Did not the prophet write, "You who are of purer eyes than to see evil and cannot look at wrong . . ." (Hab. 1:13). And the apostle says, "Christ redeemed us from the curse of the law by becoming a curse for us—for it is written, 'Cursed is everyone who is hanged on a tree'" (Gal. 3:13). Never did God so manifest *holy hatred of sin* as in the sufferings of His own beloved son! See the great glory of this mystery by faith in the spotless Lamb of God.

4. The *faithfulness* of God is plainly glorified in the cross as well. The well-known *proto-evangelium* recorded in Genesis 3:15 stated, "I will put enmity between you and the woman, and between your offspring and her offspring; he shall bruise your head, and you shall bruise his heel." The myriad of promises related to the Redeemer-Messiah find their complete and perfect fulfillment here.

5. The *love* of God is most wonderfully glorified in the cross of Christ. The familiar John 3:16 comes to mind here: "For God

so loved the world, that he gave his only Son, that whoever believes in him should not perish but have eternal life." And in 1 John 4:10 the beloved apostle adds, "In this is love, not that we loved God but that he loved us and sent his Son to be the propitiation for our sins."

The theology of the cross is of such importance that without it there can be no real Christianity. But with it there is glory and power for all who believe. A nineteenth-century American preacher stated this well:

> If, then, there may not be a less propitiation for sin than that which Christ has made, and cannot be a greater, there is but this one sacrifice. . . . It is a truth which enters deeply into the whole theory and practice of a pure Christianity. Religion in the world, religion in the heart, lives or dies with the one great expiation for sin. It is by this one great offering that men are saved, in opposition to the notion that they are saved without any propitiation at all. This great article of the Christian faith meets with no more subtle or rigorous opposition than from the unchristian thought that this redemption is needless. The foolishness of God is wiser than the reasoning pride of men.[7]

GOD HAS DEFEATED ALL HUMAN WISDOM THROUGH THE GLORY OF CHRIST CRUCIFIED

Paul succinctly summarizes, in the first chapter of his first Corinthian epistle, his apostolic commission:

> *For Christ did not send me to baptize but to preach the gospel, and not with words of eloquent wisdom, lest the cross of Christ be emptied of its power. For the word of the cross is folly to those who are perishing, but to us who are being saved it is the power of God. For it is written, "I will destroy the wisdom of the wise, and the discernment of the discerning I will thwart."*
> —vv. 17-19

I have always marveled at the challenge a physician who practices internal medicine faces in the modern world. I have two

very close friends who are internists. They are very special people. They must pay attention to every little detail. They have to ask
lots of questions. Only as the situation is clarified can the internist
make an accurate diagnosis. Other specialists are not usually
required to handle so much conflicting data. But the internist has
to cut to the chase, make a diagnosis, and then prescribe to the
patient the precise approach needed to promote the healing
process. Well, in the first eighteen verses of this letter, Paul wrote
as a competent internist. He diagnoses a serious illness in this congregation, a divisive illness that was leading to sickness and even
death (1 Cor. 11:30). When you read 1 Corinthians 1 make sure
you follow the argument carefully. Then notice that this analysis
is followed closely, logically, syntactically by the verses cited
above. The sin of the Corinthians' divisions is seen in two great
theological truths.

First, *Christ cannot be divided*. Paul asks rhetorically, "Is
Christ divided?" (1:13a). It is not possible. Christ is incapable of
division. He is one person. His church, which is His body, is also
one. Divisions based upon loyalty to human leaders cannot be tol-
erated. Why? The answer is profoundly theological, yet very simple. There is only one head, and thus there can be only one body.
To divide this body is to seek to divide Christ.

Second, *gifted teachers are not the centers of true unity in the
church*. "Was Paul crucified for you? Or were you baptized in
the name of Paul?" (v. 13b). These people were seriously defi-
cient in their understanding of Christ's purpose for them. Some
were saying, "I follow Paul." Others said, "I follow Apollos" or
"I follow Cephas." Some, apparently thinking they took the spiritual high road, said, "I follow Christ" (v. 12).

But note clearly that Paul presents the antidote to the
Corinthians' illness (vv. 17-18). In one word, it is the Gospel.
Yes, the Gospel is the antidote to this whole business. Jesus is
glorified *most* in His death by crucifixion. Thus Christ crucified is the baseline, the secure foundation, the ultimate test of

everything claiming to be Christian. This means that a church's foundation is not in its particular brand of ecclesiology. Constitutions, forms of government, visions of separation from others all make for sandy foundations for a healthy church. Churches that emphasize anything other than the glory of Christ crucified are precipitously close to spiritual peril, even if they are booming with numerical growth. Serious Christians should make this theology of the cross, not their felt needs, the reason for choosing a church home.

Further, eschatology does not create a foundation deep enough to sustain faith and godliness either. How many Christians do you know who make their views of the timing of Christ's return the bottom line for their faith?

Conservative Christians often fall into the trap of thinking that complete agreement on all matters of the faith is necessary for godliness. The great error here is that some are led to think they can articulate the deepest mysteries of the Christian faith from within a system of propositions that spells out the Christian revelation univocally—that is, with only one proper meaning. These people argue that rational minds can grasp and explain the faith with categories of thought that rest more in Aristotle and Plato than in Jesus and Paul. The mystery of the cross opposes all such thinking.

We know it is the Gospel that saves us. But do we realize that it is the Gospel that builds us up in faith and love? "Therefore, as you received Christ Jesus the Lord, so walk in him, rooted in and built up in him and established in the faith, just as you were taught, abounding in thanksgiving" (Col. 2:6-7).

In 1 Corinthians 1 Paul goes on to show the Corinthians that they do not grasp the message of the Gospel, contrasting *worldly* wisdom with *divine* wisdom. He demonstrates this by reaching back to Isaiah 29:14. Isaiah spoke of God destroying the wisdom of wise people. But what is this all about? Isaiah had seen the failure of worldly statesmanship in Judah in the face of an

Assyrian invasion. He knew this principle by having seen it at work before his very eyes. Paul thus takes this ancient divine principle and applies it. He says that in the face of the Gospel (the theology of the cross), *worldly wisdom, by necessity, utterly fails.* Then in verse 20 he poses a question: "Has not God made the wisdom of this world look foolish?" (*Phillips*). Simply put, God defeated human wisdom. But how did He do it? Through the preaching of the glory of Christ in the cross (v. 18). This is how Paul builds to a great crescendo in the first part of chapter 2.

> And I, *when I came to you, brothers, did not come proclaiming to you the testimony of God with lofty speech or wisdom. For I decided to know nothing among you except Jesus Christ and him crucified. And I was with you in weakness and in fear and much trembling, and my speech and my message were not in plausible words of wisdom, but in demonstration of the Spirit and of power, that your faith might not rest in the wisdom of men but in the power of God.*
>
> —vv. 1-5

The cross is God's power; the cross is God's wisdom. It is God's glory on earth—period. This must sink in. We must hear it afresh or we will never know spiritual health in our lives and churches. If we miss this, we miss the central glory of the revelation of God.

Again, we must see that the message of the cross is a Pauline *synonym* for the Gospel. This point is profoundly clear when Paul says he was commissioned "to preach the gospel . . . lest the cross of Christ be emptied of its power" (1:17). The glory of Christ crucified *is* the Gospel in its full and most wonderful sense. For those "being saved," the cross is "the power of God" (1:18). This text is filled with present participles. They are used here to show that these acts were going on then and there. And they are still going on here and now! Thus there are only two kinds of people in this present age—those perishing and those being saved. This same idea of the power and glory of God in the cross then and now is ubiquitously present in the New Testament (see, for example, Rom. 1:16; 1 Cor. 15:1-2; 2 Cor. 10:4-5; Gal. 6:12-14; 1 Thess. 1:4-5).

So the message of the Christian church is the message of the glory of Christ crucified; in one word, the *cross*. This is what we must glory in as followers of Jesus.

Paul doesn't stop there, as glorious as this is. He also underscores *how* we must communicate this message. I find this thrilling, but I also find it troubling in light of the present direction of most evangelical churches in North America. Paul writes:

> *For Jews demand signs and Greeks seek wisdom, but we [the apostles] preach Christ crucified, a stumbling block to Jews and folly to Gentiles, but to those who are called, both Jews and Greeks, Christ the power of God and the wisdom of God.*
> —1:22-24

And he later writes, "For I decided to know nothing among you except Jesus Christ and him crucified" (2:2).

Other things may be preparatory, but preaching is the universal apostolic method for making the glory of the cross known to believers and unbelievers alike. The good works of believers and churches can prepare the way. But even the signs and wonders of the apostles did not bring this glory into the minds and hearts of first-century Christians.

The word translated "preach" refers, simply, to public declaration through human speech. The most common use carried the idea of *public, oral* communication that both applies and persuades. Thus we see that Paul eschewed several things common to his era. He refused to use human wisdom. He did not embrace the newest styles of persuasion or the religious philosophies that might *help* the message. He stuck with the cross because the glory of God was made known by the Spirit's work.

But why is Paul so concerned here with both the *message* and the *method*? Because he saw a powerful connection between the glory of the cross as message and the glory of the message as preached. By this connection the humiliation of the Word would not be sacrificed upon some new altar of success, Corinthian or modern.

MODERN CONSEQUENCES OF LOSING THE GLORY OF THE CROSS

We have lost our center, our theological North Star. "The word of the cross" is a terse summary statement for the church in every age. Martin Luther referred to this as the *theologia crucis*, the theology of the cross. He also used the phrase *crux probat omnia* to sum up his reforming vision. Literally, this Latin phrase means "the cross is the criterion of all things." I do not think we see it this way today, at least not this clearly.

Martin Luther battled with a particular brand of medieval theology that still asserted the message of the cross. But something wasn't right about *how* the church handled this truth; thus Luther, with other evangelical Reformers, stressed the humanist idea of *ad fontes* (back to the sources). Evangelical faith demanded a return to the Bible, and in particular the languages of the Bible—namely, Hebrew and Greek. It was not enough to merely speak about the cross—it must become central. It was not enough to wear the cross or to bow before a crucifix. The message of the cross must become the key to all biblical theology. The languages of the text must be employed in service of the central message of the Bible itself. Thus Luther said on more than one occasion, "The cross *alone* is our theology."

Luther developed this theology of the cross more extensively than did any of the other writers of that era. He contrasted the *theologia crucis* with the *theologia gloriae*, a theology that saw the glory of God preeminently in the power of God in creation. Luther did not deny that we can see God's glory in creation, but he insisted that without the mystery of the cross we would soon depart from Christ-centered, revealed, biblical religion. *Theologia crucis* saw the glory of God *hidden* in the cross, yet revealed to faith. This faith is God's gift, and this faith necessarily seeks understanding. It finds understanding precisely where faith was born, in the cross of Christ.

Spurgeon saw the same idea when he said, "There is not a particle of true sanity in all the world that does not spring from the cross." Luther said, "There is not a word in the Bible which is *extra crucem*, which can be understood without reference to the cross." Charles Hodge, the nineteenth-century theologian, also saw this and said, "Whatever obscures the cross deprives the gospel of its power."

The Greek word translated "folly" in 1 Corinthians 1 is the word for "moron." It comes from the word *moria*. It literally connotes the idea of an adult with an IQ of an eight-year-old child. This word can also be connected with the Latin word *morus*, meaning "absurd." Interestingly, it was used in the Greek to describe insipid, tasteless foods. Or it was used of a physically fatigued or dull person. The *Theological Dictionary of the New Testament* (edited by Gerhard Kittel) says this word refers to "a deficiency of intellectual and spiritual capacities." The message of the church today is often insipid, dull. But this is not because we preach the glory of the cross. It is quite the opposite. We preach ourselves; we preach a message that offers to help people save their jobs, families, and homes. We have lost the message of the cross in all its foolishness.

If we would regain the message of the cross, we must have a better understanding of the nature of God. Who is God? And why was the cross necessary to save us? To answer this question we need a deeper understanding of the nature of sin and the offense that our treasonous activities have raised against a great and holy God. If the church could but understand the nature of God and the nature of man, it would never trim its sails in times such as these.

Let me illustrate what I mean by trimming our sails. One

108 THE GLORY OF CHRIST

very successful church used a series of sermons some years ago
to attract seekers. This sermon series was consciously built on
the famous "Twelve Steps" of Alcoholics Anonymous. For weeks
the pastor went through each of the steps, proclaiming that outside of the Bible there could be no better plan for getting people
ready to receive the Gospel of Christ. What do we say to this?
Well, we say what the apostle said in 1 Corinthians 1:21: "For
since, in the wisdom of God, the world did not know God through
wisdom, it pleased God through the folly of what we preach to
save those who believe." We say, with Paul, that using the wisdom
of this world does not work the work of Christ, at least not with
dependence upon the Word and Spirit. It borrows from the world
a message that it finds acceptable and substitutes it for the offensive message of the cross alone.

J. C. Ryle was surely right when he said, "As long as the world
stands, the cross will seem foolishness to natural man." And A. W.
Tozer was also right when he said, "To try to find a common
ground between the message of the cross and man's fallen reason
is to try the impossible, and if persisted in must result in an
impaired reason, a meaningless cross, and a powerless
Christianity." Ponder these words. If we continue seeking to find
common ground between the cross and the self-centered messages
of our present age, we will impair reason and end up with a meaningless cross and a powerless Christianity. I fear that is exactly
what has happened over the past fifty years or so.

We have moved away from the message of the cross and have
placed the modern emphasis upon the messenger. We live in a
culture that glories in its heroes, its stars. The message of a bloody
cross on Golgotha ("the hill of the skull") in the first century offers
nothing of star power. There is no attraction here. Is this really
happening? Yes, and much more openly than most realize. One
of the most influential church growth spokespersons, in an inter-
view several years ago, said, "Today the messenger makes the
impact, not the message." I couldn't say it more clearly than that.

But what does all this mean? Simply that the one who speaks, organizes, or leads is seen as crucial to the growth of the church. Contrast this with the words of Galatians 5:11b and 1 Corinthians 2:3-5 and ask, "Is this the way to reform the church and to pray for true revival?" Suppose for just a moment that Paul had used modern means of communication to sway the Corinthians. What would he have had at his disposal? For sure he might have had spellbinding oratory. And most definitely he could have used carefully woven arguments and appeals. The results would have been a people with a faith subject to the next change, fad, or whim or subject to the next great preacher or impressive leader.

This all came home to me several years ago when I went to a lunch seminar in the Chicago area and came face-to-face with the raw pragmatism of our time.

A minister, and I hesitate to use the term actually, was talking about drama in worship services. He was the Drama Pastor, or something like that, at his church. When it came time for questions, he prefaced this period by saying, "Do not ask me for a text to support what we do. I don't need a biblical basis. This I know, it works!" So the power of God is to be seen in contemporary light shows, well-done dramas, or even apostolic signs and wonders. No, no, no! The power of God is to be seen in a shameful cross upon which the prince of glory died two thousand years ago. Any distraction from this message is a distraction of *immensely serious* proportions. The version of Christianity this produces does several things that we should see.

First, it does not adequately believe that the Gospel is powerful enough to produce a mature faith in those who hear it and believe it. We need something more, something else. We need the props and lights and helps that make people ready to hear the Gospel. We need the atmosphere to be set so people will be enabled to believe.

What we are really saying is that the Holy Scriptures are not fully adequate for all faith and practice. We need something more. We need the Scriptures *plus* our marketing expertise.

We are also saying that the finished work of Christ is not sufficiently powerful for true evangelism. We have to have sufficient novelty and sharp means or people will not believe. This is really not new. It is the pattern embraced by revivalism from the time of Charles G. Finney (1792-1875) to the present. It has changed its garments, even becoming more sophisticated, but it is the same approach. The problem is the same—it's the message and the method *both!*

Finally, we should note that in this current message, the hope of the final day and of Christ's coming is not sufficiently comforting for those who suffer in the present age. Unless we are informed by the theology of the cross we will not glory in our sufferings and find the hope the Spirit gives to those who cling to the cross.

CONCLUSION

Charles H. Spurgeon once wisely said, "There are some sciences that may be learned by the head, but the science of Christ crucified can only be learned by the heart." The evangelical pietist Oswald Chambers understood the same reality when he said, "Every doctrine that is not embedded in the cross of Jesus will lead astray."

Let me develop a bit of theology here and show you how this works. If I were to ask, "What are the great works of Yahweh of which the Old Testament speaks?" how would you answer? If you knew your Bible you would cite great works that were the events by which Yahweh redeemed and judged His covenant people. In Deuteronomy 28 we see these works as the blessings and cursings of God upon Israel's obedience and disobedience. Daniel 3 and 6 further show that these works are the deliverances of the faithful servants of Yahweh.

Now, if you go to Acts 2 you have the record of what happened when the Holy Spirit came with power upon the infant church after Pentecost. Peter preaches (Acts 2:14-36). He rehearses the great events I have just mentioned from Deuteronomy and Daniel and cites redemptive-historical texts like Joel 2 and Psalms 16 and 110. His conclusion is quite astounding if you look at it carefully. He concludes, "Let all the house of Israel therefore know for certain that God has made him [Jesus] both Lord and Christ [Messiah], this Jesus whom you crucified" (v. 36).

The Old Testament background suggests that these words amount to Peter's saying that the works of Jesus match in significance, and indeed *exceed*, the events surrounding the Jewish exodus from Egypt.

Now do not miss the significance of this. What was central to the life and faith of Israel? The Torah, the land, the temple, and, to perhaps a slightly lesser extent, the Exodus. Peter says that Jesus fulfills the whole of these Jewish realities. As the New Testament, including later sermons in Acts, argues, *He* is the Torah, *He* is the land, and *He* is the new temple. And He accomplishes the new exodus by a much greater deliverance—His cross.

Let me put this to you another way. I do this by means of a very simple question: Is Jesus crucified the most glorious and wonderful thing you know? This is a very personal thing, and it involves divine revelation. I ask you, "Is He central? Does He come before everything else? Do you long to hear the glorious message of His cross?"

Professor James Atkinson of the University of Sheffield sums up the impact of the cross upon the world of the first century:

> It is salutary to recall that it was the cross on the hill rather than the Sermon on the Mount which produced the impact of Christianity upon the world. This message was offensive to Jew and Gentile alike, yet the early church held on to it, eventually to outlive and outthink its pagan environment.[8]

Professor Alister McGrath has seen the centrality of the cross and its glory clearly and thus writes:

> All too often the cross is relegated to one small area of Christian doctrine—how Christ gained redemption for us (soteriology)—whereas in fact it stamps an indelible and decisive impression upon every facet of the Christian faith. What does it mean for our understanding of God, of ourselves and of the world? How does it cast light on the doubt and anxiety we encounter in our lives as Christians, or the contradictions we are faced with in our existence? How does it help us wrestle with questions of doctrine, ethics, or spirituality? How does it relate to human suffering and oppression? In all these matters the mystery of the cross provides the key by which an *authentically Christian* approach to these issues may be gained.[9]

The identity of everything we hope for, everything we know, and everything we confess is bound up in the glory of the cross of our Lord Jesus Christ. A truly Christian understanding of God must begin here. Yet it also ends here, enshrouded in the mystery of this great revelation.

The famous Swiss theologian Karl Barth once said that the church was too often "trapped in the idolatry of concepts." Never was this truer than it is today for many evangelicals. But Christian faith is not primarily about concepts. At the heart of the matter it is about an *event*. The New Testament consistently directs you to this event, to this moment in real human history. It seizes you and takes you to this bloody, horrific, glorious event.

John Bowring wrote words for a familiar hymn (1825) that help us see the wonder of it all.

> *In the cross of Christ I glory,*
> *Towering o'er the wrecks of time;*
> *All the light of sacred story*
> *Gathers round its head sublime.*

When the woes of life o'ertake me,
Hopes deceive, and fears annoy,
Never shall the cross forsake me;
Lo! It glows with peace and joy.

When the sun of bliss is beaming
Light and love upon my way,
From the cross the radiance streaming
Adds more luster to the day.

Bane and blessing, pain and pleasure,
By the cross are sanctified;
Peace is there that knows no measure,
Joys that thro' all time abide.

This glory of Christ crucified is the only thing strong enough to reform and revive the church in our dark times. May God give back to both ministers and churches the message of the cross. And may we once again hear the faithful preaching of this message through the power of the Holy Spirit.

NOTES

1. I. D. E. Thomas, compiler, *The Golden Treasury of Patristic Quotations* (Oklahoma City: Hearthstone Publications, 1996), pp. 69-70.
2. Ibid., p. 68.
3. Curtis Vaughn, *A Study Guide Commentary: Galatians* (Grand Rapids, MI: Zondervan, 1972), p. 98.
4. Hans Deiter Betz, *Hermaneia Commentary on Galatians* (Philadelphia: Fortress Press, 1979), p. 269.
5. J. C. Ryle, *Expository Thoughts on the Gospels*, Vol. 7 (Cambridge, England: James Clarke & Company, repr. 1976), pp. 44-45.
6. William Hendriksen, *New Testament Commentary: The Gospel of John* (Grand Rapids, MI: Baker, 1953), p. 251.
7. Gardiner Spring, *The Attraction of the Cross* (Carlisle, PA: Banner of Truth, repr. 1983), p. 47.
8. From the foreword to Alister E. McGrath, *The Mystery of the Cross* (Grand Rapids, MI: Zondervan, 1988), p. 7.
9. Alister E. McGrath, ibid., p. 12.

6

THE GLORY OF
CHRIST'S PRESENT REIGN

JAMES I. PACKER

ONE OF CHARLES WESLEY'S best-known worship songs runs thus:

> Rejoice, the Lord is King! Your Lord and
>   King adore;
> Mortals, give thanks and sing, and
>   triumph evermore.
> Lift up your heart, lift up your voice,
> Rejoice, again I say, rejoice!
>
> Jesus, the Savior reigns, the God of truth and love;
> When he had purged our stains, he took his seat above.
> Chorus: Lift up, etc.
>
> His Kingdom cannot fail; he rules o'er earth and heaven;
> The keys of death and hell are to our Jesus given.
> Chorus: Lift up, etc.
>
> He sits at God's right hand till all his foes submit,
> And bow to his command and fall beneath his feet.
> Chorus: Lift up, etc.

Rejoice in glorious hope; Jesus the Judge shall come
And take his servants up to their eternal home.
We soon shall hear the archangel's voice,
The trump of God shall sound, Rejoice!

Wesley is celebrating the present reality and coming consummation of the heavenly reign of our Lord Jesus Christ, which is the theme of this chapter. My task is to elucidate that divine dominion in terms of its glory—that is, in terms of its praiseworthiness, by virtue of the display of deity in action that it involves. My hope and my goal is that, seeing the glory of it, we shall all be found giving God glory for it, praising, proclaiming, and adoring Christ and exulting in it in the way modeled for us by Wesley's hymn. It is the Father's will that His enthroned Son, who now has the whole world in His hands, be the center of our thoughts and our devotions and our outlook on everything as long as we are in the world (to say nothing of eternity hereafter, the larger life for which the present is preparation); and my purpose in what follows is to advance this purpose of God as best I can. For this agenda Wesley gives me a head start. Three questions that his words prompt take us straight to the heart of things.

First: What precisely is the meaning of the claim that Jesus Christ is reigning at this moment?

What is being asserted is Christ's present kingship according to the biblical sense of the word *king*; that is to say, the claim is that here and now Christ has a dominion that is sovereign and absolute, involving a full right to command and a full power to control. It was delegated to Him by the one whom the New Testament calls His God and Father (Rom. 15:6; 2 Cor. 1:3; Eph. 1:3; 1 Pet. 1:3)—a way of speaking that matches and may stem from Jesus' words to the women after His resurrection: "I am ascending to my Father and your Father, to my God and your God" (John 20:17). The Greek word for Jesus' royal reign over the world He came to save is *basileia*, which our translations render as *kingdom*. This is a familiar word in the Gospels, where Jesus teaches much about the long-awaited, long-promised kingdom of God (or to use Matthew's synonymous phrase, "kingdom of heaven") and declares that it has emerged as reality in and through His own ministry (see Luke 11:20; 16:16). Jesus preached, taught, served, and suffered as, so to speak, the king-designate in God's kingdom.

As the ascended Lord, however, He is now enthroned, and the kingdom of God—that is, the saving, judging, destiny-determining exercise of divine rule over our race—has become the kingdom of Jesus Christ. In Wesley's words, "He rules o'er earth and heaven." As He Himself put it when giving His followers their final marching orders, "All authority in heaven and on earth has been given to me" (Matt. 28:18). The sphere of His rule is explicitly called the kingdom of Christ in Colossians 1:13 and 2 Peter 1:11, and in Ephesians 5:5 it is the kingdom of Christ and God.

The present reign of Christ is thus not a territorial but a relational kingdom that becomes actual fact when humans acknowledge Jesus Christ as their king and give Him their prime loyalty in faith and obedience and love. The New Testament calls the community of those who do this the church, which is not itself the kingdom in institutional form, as has sometimes been thought, but is in the kingdom so far as it lives under the authority of the King. The universal claim of the kingdom—that is, of the King—is something that many in every generation do not know about, and it is always a main task of the church to tell them and instruct them and to use all means to lead them to accept the claim of Christ. The ongoing program of the kingdom is evangelism (whereby the church becomes global), ministry (whereby the church becomes mature), and cultural endeavor (whereby God's people labor to express Christian truth and values in family life, community relations, social service, business and politics, education and learning, fine and useful arts, pure and applied science, and all forms of life-enriching and life-renewing enterprise). The prospect for the kingdom is that one day the King will return to this world; then the full glory of the kingdom will appear, first in the re-embodiment of the dead faithful and the transformation of the living faithful so that both display the likeness of their glorified Savior, and then in the renewal of the planet—perhaps of the entire cosmos—for their endless joy with Jesus in the new Jerusalem (see Rev. 21:1-22; cf. 5). Now we know the powers and pleasures of the kingdom by faith and in foretaste; then we shall know them in all their fullness. When scholars say the kingdom is both now and not yet, this is what they mean.

At the time of Christ's return, when all will reap what they have sown in relation to Him and His kingdom, His God-given dominion will be enforced. "God has highly exalted him and bestowed on him the name that is above every name [i.e., the title *kurios*, meaning Lord, which the Greek translation of the Old Testament used for Yahweh, God Himself], so that at the name of Jesus every knee should bow . . . and every tongue confess that Jesus Christ is Lord, to the glory of God the Father" (Phil. 2:9-10). Whether with joy or with sorrow, men and angels will at that time acknowledge that from the moment of His enthronement, power to command and control has been in the hands of Jesus Christ. All along this power has been real and absolute, as it is today; but until Christ reappears it remains a hidden power, just as Christ Himself is a hidden ruler. Yet Christians know the truth about both it and Him and hence rejoice with Wesley that "his kingdom cannot fail . . . the keys of death and hell are to our Jesus given." Such, then, is Christ's dominion here and now.

Second: Whence precisely comes the knowledge of Christ's present reign? The answer, indicated already, is: from the New Testament, which is full of it.

We read over and over that Christ now sits at God's right hand. In a whole series of historical cultures, as in ordinary life today, the ceremonial placing at the right hand of the top person is a sign of executive privilege, regularly based on delegated power and responsibility. So it was, for instance, with the Grand Vizier at the ancient Persian court, and so it is with the vice-chancellor of the modern university: The person charged with the actual administration sits at the right hand of the titular ruler. And who today does not know what it means to describe a person as someone else's right-hand man? Now, this is the position in relation to God the Father that the New Testament tells us Jesus was given at His ascension to heaven, and which remains His until He returns. The repetition of this in the letter to the Hebrews, in particular, is so frequent as to have almost a drumbeat effect. "After making purification for sins, he sat down at the right hand of the Majesty on high" (1:3). "To which of the angels has he [God] ever said, 'Sit at my right hand until I make your enemies a footstool for your feet'?" (1:13, citing Ps. 110:1). "We have . . . a high priest . . . who is seated at the right hand of the throne of the Majesty in heaven" (8:1). "When Christ had offered for all time a single sacrifice for sins, he sat down at the right hand of God, waiting from that time until his enemies should be made a footstool for his feet" (10:12-13). "Let us run with endurance the race that is set before us, looking to Jesus, the founder and perfecter of our faith, who for the joy that was set before him endured the cross, despising the shame, and is seated at the right hand of the throne of God" (12:1-2). Addressing Jewish converts who were harassed, unsettled, confused, and toying with the idea of returning to Judaism, the writer rubs his reader's noses, as it were, in the fact that the Lord Jesus, the Son of God, their great and only high priest, now occupies a place of delegated royalty and sovereign power, from which He helps his servants to stand firm.

Paul's Christ, too, is "seated at the right hand of God" (Col. 3:1; also Rom. 8:34; Eph. 1:20), as is the Christ of the longer ending of Mark (16:19) and of 1 Peter 3:22, which adds the detail "with angels, authorities, and powers having been subjected to him." And in Revelation 3:21 Jesus promises, "The one who

conquers, I will grant him to sit with me on my throne, as I also
conquered and sat down with my Father on his throne." The testimony is emphatic, unanimous, and abundant: The Lord Jesus
is indeed king.

Third: Who and what precisely is this Jesus Christ, the reigning Lord? This question needs to be asked and answered at the
outset, for it would not be right to focus on the kingdom in a
way that displaces the King from the forefront of our minds.
That would move us away from the Jesus-centeredness of the New
Testament and so undermine our faith, praise, growth, joy, and
weight as witnesses. I offer now, therefore, before attempting to
take the kingdom theme any further, a mini-Christology; and as
a basis for this, I now cite Paul's classic Christological utterance
in Colossians 1:15-20, where, having declared that God the Father
"transferred us to the kingdom of his beloved Son, in whom we
have redemption, the forgiveness of sins" (vv. 13-14), he goes on
to say of the Son:

> He is the image of the invisible God, the firstborn of all cre-
> ation. For by him all things were created, in heaven and on
> earth, visible and invisible, whether thrones or dominions or
> rulers or authorities—all things were created through him and
> for him. And he is before all things, and in him all things hold
> together. And he is the head of the body, the church. He is the
> beginning, the firstborn from the dead, that in everything he
> might be preeminent. For in him all the fullness of God was
> pleased to dwell, and through him to reconcile to himself all
> things, whether on earth or in heaven, making peace by the
> blood of his cross.

In light of this passage, and of the rest of the New Testament
that surrounds it, I formulate my sketch of the glory of Jesus
Christ, the divine King in the divine kingdom, as follows:

PERMANENT IMAGE AND PERMANENT CENTRALITY

The Son is the second of three distinct yet identical persons, consubstantial, coequal, coeternal, and cooperating, within the mystery of the complex unity—the tri-unity, or Trinitarian unity, as one may choose to say—of God's being. In terms of character and powers—attributes, if we wish to use the old word—the Son is eternally and unchangeably the *image*, or perfect match, of the Father in every respect (Col. 1:15; 2 Cor. 4:4; Heb. 1:3). In terms of personhood, the Father and the Son each exist "in" the other (John 10:38; 14:10-11; 17:21), so that "I and the Father are one" (John 10:30) and "Whoever has seen me has seen the Father" (14:9); this is Christ's own witness to the mystery of their consubstantiality. In terms of cooperation with the Father (the reality labeled by older theologians as the divine *economy*), the Son is the *Word*, the Logos, the personal expression and executant of all the Father's purposes in creation, providence, and grace. When Paul calls Him "the firstborn of all creation" (Col. 1:15), he means, as verse 17 shows, that the Son existed prior to any of the things that were made through His agency. The catalogue of creatures covers a vast variety of objects and life-forms and a vast range of not only human but also angelic intelligences (v. 16); and the staggering, breathtaking truth is that every single item in the cosmos owes not only its origin but also its continuing existence to the one whom we know as Jesus Christ (v. 17). It is in Christ that "all things hold together" (v. 17); He "upholds the universe by the word of his power" (Heb. 1:3). Without the upholding action of the Word, everything that now is, ourselves included, would simply cease to be.

Nor is this all. In terms, finally, of the divine program for this world and the next, it is the Father's pleasure to exalt the Son as the *focus* of all cosmic life and creaturely worship forever. All things were created, and the church was redeemed and brought into active being as His body, not only by Him but "for him" (v. 16)—that is, so that in all things He might be "preeminent" (v.

18)—"Christ Supreme," as an unforgettable Bible exposition put it to me when I was searching just eight days before Christ Himself broke into my life and drew me to Himself. The Father "loves the Son" and wills that "all may honor the Son, just as they honor the Father" (John 5:20, 23). This Son-centered focus of all God's plans to all eternity gives us the proper perspective, the angle of vision we need, for studying the specifics that we survey now.

PERMANENT HUMANITY AND PERMANENT HEADSHIP

To fulfill God's plan of grace for the salvation of sinners, the Word became flesh, adding to himself *humanity* without the least diminution of His eternal divinity. As the God-man He became the Mediator, man for God and God for man, dealing with each as advocate and spokesman for the other, bringing together the Father, alienated from our race through our preference for sin, and ourselves, alienated from God for the same reason. The Son's mediatorial role led Him down to depths of humiliation and agony on His sin-bearing cross, then up from the grave to heights of exaltation and joy. This was achieved through resurrection for a further forty-day ministry to His disciples, followed by ascension to heaven, there to reign as the glorified Messiah until the time set for His reappearance on earth. We may properly speak of this as the Son's two-stage journey home. The Apostles' Creed (a universally accepted confession of faith that seems to have begun life in the second century as a syllabus for catechetical instruction) tells the story succinctly like this:

> . . . Born of the Virgin Mary, Suffered under Pontius Pilate, Was crucified, dead, and buried: He descended into hell [Hades, the place of departed spirits; the statement simply confirms that Jesus truly died]; The third day he rose again from the dead; He ascended into heaven, and sitteth on the right hand of God the Father Almighty; From thence he shall come to judge the quick [living] and the dead. (*Anglican Prayer Book* version)

Throughout the period from Christ's first to His second coming, His threefold messianic ministry continues—as prophet, revealing and teaching through His Word and Spirit; as priest, interceding—that is, intervening in our interest—on the basis of His once-for-all atoning sacrifice; and as king, directing, pardoning, judging, and rewarding His people while protecting them providentially from evil and ruin. Believers who receive this threefold ministry with responsive hearts constitute the church, and the church, so Paul tells us, is the body of which Christ is the head (Col. 1:18; 2:19). *Headship* means this threefold messianic ministry plus Christ's life-giving, faith-sustaining, growth-inducing work in us through His Spirit. Authority, guidance, enabling, and enriching are all aspects of the head-to-body service that Christ renders to His church. Both Christ's *humanity* and His *headship* are permanent realities that will continue until His return and beyond.

All the things mentioned thus far may be spoken of matter-of-factly, for they are in truth matters of fact; but they must always be thought about with deepest reverence and humility—"with awe, and wonder, and with bated breath," to quote a noble hymn—for this is the most startling and mysterious set of facts that has ever come before the human mind. Everything here is unique, supernatural, miraculous, and incomprehensible in the old sense, meaning that there is more to it all than our limited minds can grasp. A supernatural entrance into this world (virginal conception and birth) and a supernatural exit from it (resurrection from death and ascension); a supernatural identity whereby, without querying the belief that there is one God only, a man is to be recognized as a second divine person, God with God coming to us as God from God; supernatural works of loving power, benefiting great numbers of the needy; then a supernatural transaction whereby the second divine person sacrificed Himself to the first divine person, enduring the retributive hell due to humans; and now a supernatural presence whereby the second divine person, having returned to the first divine person in heaven, meets, calls, and changes men and women on earth through the agency of a third divine person—these are the incomprehensible, seemingly incredible, yet really indubitable facts with which Christianity confronts the world.

Believers know that all this is actual, for the Bible declares it consistently, and the rational case for faith is overwhelming; but nobody can explain how any of it is possible—how, as we may put it, these things can be. Though the meaning of the facts is clear and the reasons to believe are compelling, the facts themselves remain mind-boggling and mysterious. Small wonder that Greeks in the apostolic age dismissed the Gospel as wild foolishness! And as if the realities reviewed thus far were not enough, yet more mysteries await us as we complete our survey of biblical Christology.

PERMANENT UNION AND PERMANENT COMMUNION

Self-centeredness is natural to sinners such as we all are, and it comes out as much in our mental as in our relational attitudes; so man-centered, self-absorbed accounts of the saving work of God are common among Christian people. But the view of salvation that the New Testament writers model when they explore the subject, though full on personal application and experience, is God-centered and Christ-centered and doxologically oriented throughout. Its focus is not on us who receive salvation, but on God who planned it and on Christ who makes it ours by incorporating us into Himself so that we share His risen life. Union and communion are the two sides of this sharing.

Union with Christ, so as to be "in" Christ in the New Testament sense, is a spiritual mystery. In a real yet inconceivable way, through the agency of the Holy Spirit who comes from heaven to indwell us, the risen, ascended, glorified Lord establishes a vital link and bond of life (that is, of responsive energy) between Himself on His throne and us believers below. Within this linkage the reconstructing of us in Christ's image starts at once, with the creative renewal of the motivational and expressive core of the believer's being—what Scripture regularly calls the *heart*—so that his or her deepest desire and inner drive is now gratefully and adoringly to love, serve, obey, please, honor, exalt, glorify, and enjoy God—a totally different mind-set from the self-centeredness that ruled before. When Paul rebutted the Corinthians' view of him as crazy by explaining that "the love of Christ controls us . . . if anyone is in Christ, he is a new creation" (2 Cor. 5:14, 17), it was this remaking of the heart that he had in view.

The theology of the union is explained in Romans 6:3-11, Colossians 2:11-14, and Titus 3:4-7 in terms of how water is used in baptism: Having gone under it, either by being immersed or by having it poured or sprinkled on them, the candidates, now symbolically cleansed, leave the water behind. Going under signifies death and burial with Christ in Christ—in other words, the closure of the self-centered, guilty, unworthy life one was living before. Going forward after that signifies that one has started a new life with Christ in Christ, a life increasingly conformed in motive and attitude to Christ's own life, both before and since His resurrection. Salvation, both positional and transformational—reconciliation and justification, pardon and forgiveness, adoption and hope of heaven, present peace and promised preservation, together with regeneration of heart, formation in us of Christlike character and holy habits, empowering for mortification of sin, progressive and final glorification—is from start to finish through Christ, with Christ, in Christ. As was strikingly said in the memorable Bible exposition that I mentioned earlier, "What God wants in our lives is more of his Son." The meaning of our union with Christ could hardly be better put. And once it is established, it lasts for all eternity. When Christ has joined us to Himself in this sharing of resurrection life, He never lets us go. "I give them eternal life, and they will never perish, and no one will snatch them out of my hand" (John 10:28).

Faith-communion expresses this supernatural union in our

ongoing life. Communion with God the Father and with His Son
Jesus Christ is a reality embracing all praises, all prayers, all light
of understanding and joy of assurance that the Father and the
Son bestow, and all conscious experiences of the gracious divine
presence with us. All our life in Christ is to be lived with Christ
as companion, under Christ as Master, to Christ as our lover
whom we must always be seeking to please, and for Christ in the
sense of purposefully fulfilling His goals and advancing His glory.
And the book of Revelation paints ecstatic word-pictures of this
fellowship of worship and service continuing and deepening in
heaven after God's people have left this world behind.

Union and communion have much to do with the kingdom
of Christ, which indeed is precisely the personal, salvific, regen-
erative, transformational form of His communion with those
drawn into union with Him as described above. Paul's letters to
the Colossians and Ephesians make this particularly clear.
Colossians was written to counter the idea that salvation is not
through Christ alone but through Christ plus some kind of angelic
ministry, and Ephesians seems to be a circular letter growing out
of Colossians. Both letters are celebrations of union and communion with Christ throughout. In the Colossians passage quoted
earlier, Paul presented God's beloved Son as co-creator and universal sustainer, who in incarnation embodied the divine "fullness" (v. 19; clearly a Colossian tag-word that Paul takes over
for his own purposes) and became the reconciling reintegrator of
the cosmos through his peacemaking blood-shedding for sins on
the cross.

Paul then declares the Gospel to be a revealed "mystery," in
the sense of a divine secret that without revelation would not be
known at all (not quite the theologians' use of the word), and he
dwells on "how great . . . are the riches of the glory of this mystery, which is Christ in you, the hope of glory" (1:26-27). In this
way he works up to the letter's central admonition: "As you
received Christ Jesus the Lord, so walk in him, rooted and built up

in him and established in the faith, just as you were taught, abounding in thanksgiving" (2:6-7). What "received" and "walk" mean here in terms of union and communion with Christ, whereby the former Christless, sinful life ends and a new life in and with Christ begins, is then explained (see 2:10-14, 20; 3:1-4, 10-11, 17 [and note the use of "in the Lord" in 4:7, 17]). The same union-and-communion frame shapes the message of Ephesians, where "in" (in the phrases "in Christ" and "in the Lord") is from our present standpoint the key word of the whole letter (see 1:3-4; 2:4-10, 13-22; 3:4-6, 11, 16-21; 4:15-16; 5:8-21; 6:21).

So Jesus Christ, the divine Son, the second person of the triune Godhead, is right at the center of all that the twenty-seven books of the New Testament are concerned to set forth. The basic apostolic message is that salvation is in Christ, through Christ, with Christ, and for Christ: He is the Savior and the Lord, who at His Father's will came to earth as the one and only God-man in order to save us, and we sinners find salvation through letting our ongoing life story become part of His ongoing life story. Union and communion with Christ thus constitute the foundational theme, the ground bass of the passacaglia, we might say, from the beginning to end of the apostolic writings. Each New Testament author is his own man and has his own way of saying these things, but analysis shows that each one views Christ's saving ministry within this Christ-centered, union-and-communion frame; and whether or not they speak of Christ's kingdom directly, they are all aiming to show how people should relate to the fact that Jesus Christ is the Lord, the hands-on ruler of everything, now reigning from His heavenly throne.

It helps at this point to note that the kingdom of God, which is the present kingdom of Christ, has a history. It became fact and was made known by stages, progressively. According to the prophets' predictions, God was to set up a bigger and better Davidic dominion, bringing *shalom* (peace)—good relationships on earth, stemming from a good relationship with God; a state of fulfillment, well-being, contentment, and joy beyond anything that the world had known before. (*Shalom* really does mean all of this; the word expresses more than any one English term can carry.) This was what the prophets' visions of welfare and prosperity signified, and it began to become reality through Jesus' ministry prior to His cross. According to the evangelists' narratives, those who entrusted to Jesus their destiny and became His followers and disciples as He traveled and taught in Palestine tasted this *shalom*, or eternal life as Jesus began to call it, straightaway. Little as they grasped at first of what Jesus was telling them about the kingdom and His own place in it, they gave Him their own full loyalty, and this established for them the relationship with Jesus through which this *shalom* was, and is, bestowed.

According to the book of Acts and the apostles' letters, however, from the day of Pentecost onward the doctrine of salvation through Christ the Lord became increasingly clear through revelation and was increasingly well understood, and soon Paul in particular was explicitly declaring that salvation through Christ is salvation in Christ, covenantally, relationally, vitally, and transformatively, through election, calling, reconciliation, justification, and glorification—to echo Paul's main technical terms for explaining what union and communion with Christ amount to. John, James, and Jude do not really have a technical vocabulary, while Peter and the writer to the Hebrews have their own; but union and communion with Christ, deepening and unending, is what they are all concerned to spell out as truth for the mind, joy for the heart, hope for the future, and a tonic for living each day. Like Paul, they present this as the main thing the Gospel is about.

So far we have been reflecting on how the heavenly reign of our Lord Jesus Christ touches individuals; how, we next ask, does it bear on the church? I have claimed that promoting union and communion with the world's true ruler is the central concern of all New Testament writers. Often in the past, however, I, with

many others, have identified the health of the church as their tar-
get. Is there a contradiction here? If not, what is the connection?
To show the connection, I now say four things.

First, the entire plan of grace, in which the Lord Jesus is mediator, testator, executor, and administrator throughout, has as its
goal the perfecting of the church. The church, God's covenant
community, sharing in all the stages of the history of the kingdom,
is defined for us in the New Testament as Christ's body, building,
and bride, and Christ, we are told, intends to "present the church
to himself in splendor, without spot or wrinkle or any such thing,
that she might be holy and without blemish" (Eph. 5:27). This is
how our union-and-communion relationship with Him will be
finally fulfilled.

Second, Christ the cosmic king, to whom all authority in
heaven and earth has been given, is the church's Lord, just as He
is its life. The church, both local and universal, is called to be the
expression and as such the agent of Christ's kingdom, shaped by
the grace of it, spreading the knowledge of it through believers'
words and deeds, and standing under the judgment of it when
disbelief and sin cloud its worship, witness, and work in the
world. Always and everywhere the church, the professed Christian
community, must answer to Christ for its own inner quality.

Third, individual Christians are not to think of themselves as
if they are, so to speak, the only pebble on God's beach. They
should know that their corporate, communal, churchly identity
is from God's standpoint the basic truth about them. They are
adopted children in the Father's great family, brothers and sisters
of Christ (Heb. 2:11-13); they are members of Christ, that is
units—limbs, organs, body parts—in the great structure of the
true temple where God dwells through the Spirit, crowning the
gatherings of His own people with the gift of His own felt presence (1 Cor. 3:16-17; cf. 14:23-25; Eph. 2:19-22); and it is in these
terms that they must regard themselves. Union and communion
are certainly to be pursued individually, but never individualisti-

cally. There is no place for spiritual lone rangers under the kingship of Jesus Christ. Those united to and communing with Him belong in the church.

Fourth, in all the church's ministrations Christ Himself is the true minister, teaching, evangelizing, shepherding, nurturing, energizing, and equipping, and we who serve must see ourselves simply as His tools—His hands, feet, voice, smile, the embodied expression of His love—whom from time to time He is pleased to use in His own work of building His church. Proper humility as we labor for God springs from seeing that He does not need us and could get on without us, so that it is a huge privilege to be taken as tools for His tasks. Many of us, I think, cherish conceit that needs to be punctured at this point. As Richard Baxter, the Puritan, lay dying, a visitor burbled appreciation of his writings (and he was perhaps the most masterful, certainly the most voluminous writer on practical Christianity that Britain ever produced). In reply, Baxter whispered, "I was but a pen in the hand of God; and what praise is due a pen?" That models what I mean.

Jesus said, "I have other sheep. . . . I must bring them also," and also "I, when I am lifted up from the earth, will draw all people to myself" (John 10:16; 12:32). How did He envisage doing it? How does He do it today (for He does it still)? Answer: through Christians communicating the Gospel. That, Paul means his Gentile readers in Asia Minor to understand, was how after achieving reconciliation with God for them, Christ "came and preached peace to you who were far off" (Eph. 2:17). And of his own missionary ministry, Paul wrote, "I will not venture to speak of anything except what Christ has accomplished through me to bring the Gentiles to obedience—by word and deed, by the power of signs and wonders, by the power of the Spirit of God" (Rom. 15:18-19). This is how Christ fulfills His statement of intent in Matthew 16:18, "I will build my church."

Building means upbuilding. Explaining the spiritual growth of the church through life together, Paul writes of "Christ, from whom the whole body, joined and held together by every joint with which it is equipped, when each part is working properly, makes the body grow so that it builds itself up in love" (Eph. 4:15-16). He has in view not only people using their spiritual gifts, both of speech and of Samaritan-type service (see the list in Rom. 12:6-8), but also Christ using their ministry to mature His church. Christ, then, once more is the body-builder, and we, once more, are His tools.

Giftedness, be it said, is not necessarily a sign of either union or communion with Christ; but integral to the pursuit of a full-scale personal link with Jesus Christ is a quest for the welfare of the church. The New Testament books were written to advance this twofold goal, and Christians' lives are to be lived with the same double purpose.

Christ's ministry to His church includes the empowering of the consciously weak to stand firm under pressure. This is His inter-cession for them, or intervention on their behalf, as the Greek might better be rendered (Rom. 8:34; Heb. 7:25). His asking the Father appears as part of it (cf. John 14:16 with v. 26; 15:26 with 16:7); but we should note, first, that the asking is the act of a reign-ing sovereign, not of a suppliant without standing; second, that the intervention covers not just asking that the weak be helped but actually helping them (see Heb. 4:16); and, third, that Christ's redeeming death for them secured His right to help them any way they need as they travel to the glory they are now to inherit.

All along I have been assuming and, indeed, affirming that being a Christian means not just embracing orthodoxy about the atonement, but living under Christ the Savior as one's Lord, which is the relationship to which true faith leads. Perhaps it is in order here, as I close, to affirm my amazement that Bible-believers should ever have doubted that this is what the Gospel calls us to as the way of life and salvation. My impression, however, is that doubts about "Lordship salvation," as the critics of the biblical Gospel called it, are rapidly fading away, and I am glad; for there

could be no reformation or revival, and no adequate honoring of
the Christ who reigns or adequate discipleship to Him as long as
these doubts held sway.

So to conclude: The messianic reign that the Father has delegated to our Lord Jesus is a fact with which all mankind needs to
come to terms. Christ has the right and the power to command
everyone, to control everything, and to claim dominion over every
life-activity. As Abraham Kuyper classically put it, there is no
square inch of reality of which the Lord Jesus does not say,
"Mine!" At this time Christ's kingdom is defied by Satan and his
hosts and denied by over two-thirds of the human race, and much
of the King's power is kept in reserve, for reasons that have not
been shared with us. But the final triumph of the kingdom is
promised and certain. Paul speaks of it thus in 1 Corinthians 15:

> *Then comes the end, when he delivers the kingdom to God
> the Father after destroying every rule and every authority and
> power. For he must reign until he has put all his enemies under
> his feet. The last enemy to be destroyed is death. For "God
> has put all things in subjection under his feet." . . . When all
> things are subjected to him, then the Son himself will also be
> subjected to him who put all things in subjection under him,
> that God may be all in all.*
>
> —vv. 24-28

Observe: (1) Death will be abolished when Jesus returns to
raise all the dead for judgment, to receive His risen and perfected
church to Himself, and to renew the cosmic order. (2) Christ will
deliver up the messianic kingdom to the Father by completing its
agenda of judgment and salvation and establishing *shalom*. For all
eternity He will continue to be the Son reigning with the Father
and the Spirit, but the era of specifically messianic rule to complete
God's saving purpose by applying redemption to all the redeemed
will have come to an end. (3) Until that consummation, conflict
with evil and untruth will continue. Satan will not give up as
long as he is allowed to go on.

But Christ has conquered; His cross was the road to His crown; it is His glory ever to reign in glory, and it is our glory ever to give Him glory on that account. *Glory be to thee, O Lord.*

We listened to Charles Wesley as our study opened; let us hear him again as it closes, meditating this time on Jesus' story of the bridesmaids in Matthew 25:

> *Ye slumbering souls, arise! With all the dead awake;*
> *Unto salvation wise, oil in your vessels take.*
> *Upstarting at the midnight cry,*
> *"Behold the heavenly bridegroom nigh."*
>
> *He comes, he comes to call the nations to his bar,*
> *And take to glory all who meet for glory are:*
> *Made ready for your free reward,*
> *Go forth with joy to meet your Lord.*
>
> *Ye that have here received the unction from above,*
> *And in his Spirit lived, and thirsted for his love,*
> *Jesus shall claim you for his bride;*
> *Rejoice with all the sanctified.*
>
> *Rejoice in glorious hope of that great day unknown,*
> *When you shall be caught up to stand before his throne;*
> *Called to partake the marriage feast,*
> *And lean on our Immanuel's breast.*
>
> *The everlasting doors shall soon the saints receive,*
> *Above yon angel powers in glorious joy to live;*
> *Far from a world of grief and sin,*
> *With God eternally shut in.*

Amen!

7

THE GLORY OF
CHRIST'S COMING AGAIN

R. ALBERT MOHLER, JR.

FRANK KERMODE, an influential literary critic, wrote a book based on some of his lectures entitled *The Sense of an Ending.*[1] In it, Kermode argued that human existence demands the sense of an ending. Just as literature is meaningless without the horizon of an ending in sight, so too, Kermode argued, human existence demands the knowledge that an end is coming for our satisfaction emotionally. Interestingly, however, Kermode made these observations without assurance that any kind of particular end is in view.

In the year 1999 we went through a period of millennial expectation. We remember the Y2K crisis and the fear, expressed by some, that an apocalyptic ending was coming with the turn of the calendar from December 31, 1999, to January 1, 2000. Some suggested that an imminent economic, technological, political, and ecological crisis could be upon us. Admittedly, even those of us who thought that was overblown nevertheless watched the turning of the digits quite carefully, wondering if the lights would go out, or worse.

We are told that the kind of apocalyptic expectation that marked the end of the second millennium is nothing like that which marked the end of the first. There is good historical literature about the sense of millennial expectation and eschatological anticipation of an imminent apocalypse that marked the turn from the year 999 to 1000. Part of this likely stems from the fact that we feel so comfortable now, so satisfied economically and technologically.

Neil Postman has argued that meaning in this culture is very difficult to separate from the meaningless.[2] That is, the media culture has shaped our minds to expect a pattern of one thing after another separated by the formula "and now . . ." It appears to us that if we were to know the end of the world was at hand and the Lord was about to return, the TV anchor would simply say, "Coming up next, the end of the world as we know it, but first this message from our sponsors."

We need to unthink the thinking of the world by being confronted with the Word of God. Indeed, we need to be confronted in such a way that we rethink even what we think we know about the coming of the Lord, so that we might learn to seek Christ's glory in His coming.

Sadly, it appears that most evangelical Christians think that the return of our Lord is primarily about *us*. It does not take much more than a brief glance at the evangelical literature and sermons of our day to confirm this. So far as many of them are concerned, this is a story about us—in particular, the fact that we are of such worthiness that Christ is going to come back to claim us.

The biblical perspective is quite different, however. It does not deny that we are Christ's purchased possession, that He will indeed return to claim His own, or that He, as the firstfruits of the resurrection, will be followed by all those who are in Christ. But it does make clear that these other truths are established in God's own glory. Accordingly, we see that God does what He does, in the first place, for the sake of the increase of His own glory. When the Lord Jesus comes, He will come for the ultimate and eternal purpose of glorifying Himself and glorifying the Father.

As evangelicals, we face the danger of treating references to God's glory too casually. Such references occur frequently in our hymns, and they are peppered throughout our evangelical conversation. Sadly, however, it has become all too easy for these words to fall out of our mouths without rendering any specific meaning. Let us be clear about that which we speak when we mention something as great as the glory of God.

To that end, we must recall that when we speak of God's glory, we should think of two dimensions. On the one hand, God's glory is to be understood in terms of an *intrinsic reality*. On the other hand, God's glory can also be spoken of in terms of its *external manifestation*. Now, in terms of the intrinsic reality—in God's inherent Godness—God neither waxes nor wanes in glory, for He is infinite glory in and of Himself. And yet, in the external manifestation the Lord's glory can increase. He can cause us to see it more visibly and experience Him more directly.

Let us think through the entirety of salvation history in terms of God's glory. In the first place, God enjoys His eternal glory. He created the cosmos and the world as the theater of His own glory. He created human beings as His image-bearers to reflect His glory. In our rebellion, we sinned against Him. And what was the core of our sin? It was an effort to rob God of His rightful glory and claim it for ourselves. But God is jealous of His glory— He will not tolerate the thievery of it. He must punish those who would rob Him of His glory. And yet He determined to glorify Himself by sending Jesus Christ, of whom it is said, "we saw His glory, glory as of the only begotten from the Father, full of grace and truth" (John 1:14).[3]

We also see that Christ's mediatorial death and resurrection were accomplished to God's glory. And by God's marvelous grace, sinners are gloriously saved by the cross. We are told that Christ will bring many sons to glory. We are told that even now we should await His coming in glory. Thereafter He will reign in glory, and we will be glorified in such a way that we can properly and eternally represent God's glory.

The glory of Christ and His coming. What in the world are we to do with this? Jonathan Edwards spoke of "sinners in the hands of an angry God." Perhaps we should repent of "eschatology in the hands of clever evangelicals." There is around us a "rapture mania." For many evangelicals, eschatology is a hobby, complete with charts, graphs, timetables, and an inordinate interest in the European Common Market—now called the European Economic Community.

Mark Noll, at Wheaton College, has suggested that this kind of mental game playing is an evidence of a lack of evangelical seriousness.[4] Perhaps it would be more appropriately deemed a lack of evangelical faithfulness. It is certainly a failure to understand what the Bible teaches about the glory of Christ's coming.

On the other hand, for the Protestant left, eschatology has become nothing more than a metaphor. Thus we see the theological evasion of a Jürgen Moltmann and Wolfhart Pannenberg, in which history is pointed toward a metaphorical future, and any kind of historical return is either redefined or apparently denied. All meaning is pushed into the future, in the hope of an eschatological reality.

We need biblical correction, and on this matter we will find help by looking at Hebrews 9:24-28.

> *For Christ did not enter a holy place made with hands, a mere copy of the true one, but into heaven itself, now to appear in the presence of God for us; nor was it that He would offer Himself often, as the high priest enters the holy place year by year with blood that is not his own. Otherwise, He would have needed to suffer often since the foundation of the world; but now once at the consummation of the ages He has been manifested to put away sin by the sacrifice of Himself. And inasmuch as it is appointed for men to die once and after this comes judgment, so Christ also, having been offered once to bear the sins of*

many, will appear a second time for salvation without reference
to sin, to those who eagerly await Him.

Certainly this reminds us of Christ's glory as our substitutionary mediator. As our great High Priest, He offered not the blood of an animal, but shed His own blood for the remission of our sins. In so doing, He entered a tabernacle not made with human hands, but the holy of holies in heaven itself. There, He did not perform a sacrifice that would be repeated annually or wash us only externally. Rather, He performed that sacrifice which purchased our salvation—an eternal, once-for-all atonement that cleanses us without and transforms us within.

But now, in this same chapter, the writer of Hebrews very clearly points us to the fact of Christ's coming. Let us see, first of all, that Christ is coming *in reality*.[5] According to Scripture, this is an assured fact, a certain promise. He is coming, and when He comes, it will be an event in the space-time continuum of history. Indeed, it will be a visible return in His resurrection body.

Jesus Himself affirmed His future visible return in Matthew 26:64 saying, "hereafter you will see the Son of Man sitting at the right hand of power, and coming on the clouds of heaven." This expectation is repeated in Acts 1:10-11 where Luke reports that "as they were gazing intently into the sky while He was going, behold, two men in white clothing stood beside them. They also said, 'Men of Galilee, why do you stand looking into the sky? This Jesus, who has been taken up from you into heaven, will come in just the same way as you have watched Him go into heaven.'"

Paul Davies, a leading cosmologist and scientist, has written a book entitled *The Last Three Minutes*.[6] It is part of a trilogy, in which he speaks about the first three minutes of creation—an interesting narrative for one who was not there. Nonetheless, he posits a thesis concerning how the beginning might have occurred. In order to bring his systematic scientific treatise to a close, he must now speak about the end, and so he writes about the last three minutes as well. Suffice it to say that it is not a pretty sight, cosmologically speaking. According to Davies, the natural world simply runs out of energy and dies a natural death.

Those who are committed to such a naturalistic view of the universe believe that all creation came together because of the chance encounter of time, space, matter, and energy. Given the second law of thermodynamics, order will lead to disorder, being to non-being, and energy to entropy; then everything that now exists will head into simple non-being. The transformation of non-being to being was explosive, they tell us; but according to these cosmologists, the transformation of being into non-being is going to be more explosive still—black holes, antimatter, asteroids, radiation belts, the collapse of being into non-being, an atomic catastrophe, a metaphysical meltdown of epic proportions.

But it is not just the cosmologists. Some of the ecologists would also have us think that the world is about to collapse into non-being, because of ecological misuse and global warming, etc. No doubt, the end is coming, but it is not that kind of an end. Surely we must be responsible stewards, but it is not within our power to bring the cosmos to a conclusion. Nor will we find the world simply dissipating itself by the endless progression of entropy into non-being. *He* will come! Christ is Lord over all time and creation, and in due time He will return. In Hebrews 9:28 we learn that Christ will appear a second time for salvation, and in His appearing He will be recognized for who He is.

Charles Spurgeon put it this way:

> Nor will there merely be a difference in his coming; there will be a most distinct and apparent difference *in his person*. He will be the same, so that we shall be able to recognize him as the Man of Nazareth, but O how changed! Where now the carpenter's smock? Royalty hath now assumed its purple. Where now the toil-worn feet that needed to be washed after their long journeys of mercy? They are sandaled with light, they "are like unto fine brass as if they burned in a furnace." Where now

the cry, "Foxes have holes and the birds of the air have nests, but I, the Son of Man, have not where to lay My head"? Heaven is his throne; earth is his foot-stool. Methinks in the night visions, I behold the day dawning. And to the Son of Man there is given dominion, and glory, and a kingdom, that all people, nations, and languages, should serve him. Ah! who would think to recognize in the weary man and full of woes, the King eternal, immortal, invisible. Who would think that the humble man, despised and rejected, was the seed-corn out of which there should grow that full corn in the ear, Christ all-glorious, before whom the angels veil their faces and cry, "Holy, Holy, Holy, Lord God of Sabaoth!" He is the same, but yet how changed! Ye that despised him, will ye despise him now?[7]

The Lord is coming in reality. His bodily return is not merely a theological metaphor; it is a biblical promise. The Lord's coming is not something to be negotiated away, any more than it is to be plotted on timetables. God's faithful should anticipate Christ's return in the full knowledge that His coming bears the stamp of His own promise, and indeed His own warning that we should live in expectation of His return and prepare ourselves for His coming.

Not only is Christ coming in reality, He is also coming *in authority*. In His coming, He will be revealed as king. We can put in contrast the lowly manger of Bethlehem and the throne from which Christ now reigns. When the Lord Jesus Christ returns, there will be no doubt that He comes as king to rule.

In Revelation 19:11-16 the apostle John provided a foretaste of Christ's eschatological coming, saying:

And I saw heaven opened, and behold, a white horse, and He who sat on it is called Faithful and True, and in righteousness He judges and wages war. His eyes are a flame of fire, and on His head are many diadems; and He has a name written on Him which no one knows except Himself. He is clothed with a robe dipped in blood, and His name is called The Word of God. And the armies which are in heaven, clothed in fine linen,

*white and clean, were following Him on white horses. From
His mouth comes a sharp sword, so that with it He may strike
down the nations, and He will rule them with a rod of iron; and
He treads the wine press of the fierce wrath of God, the
Almighty. And on His robe and on His thigh He has a name
written, "KING OF KINGS, AND LORD OF LORDS."*

We will know that He is coming as king and that He will
establish His rule. This relativizes all earthly kings and king-
doms. This is the ultimate relativizer of all the claims ever made by
all of the despots, presidents, and princes throughout history.
For then we will see who is the King, and He will reign in glory.
All the kings of the earth shall bow before Him.

This affirms the necessity of understanding Christ's *present*
reign in His sovereignty, as well as the manifestation of that reign
in the universal knowledge that will take place at His return. Upon
His return He will take control of all things visibly, undeniably,
and uncontestably. He will rule with a rod of iron, and He will
be seen as King of kings and Lord of lords. This is active sovereignty, not passive; it is total, not partial; it is unconditional, not
conditional.

Consider 1 Corinthians 15:24-28:

*Then comes the end when He hands over the kingdom to the
God and Father, when He has abolished all rule and all authority and power. For He must reign until He has put all His enemies under His feet. The last enemy that will be abolished is
death. For He has put all things in subjection under His feet.
But when He says, "All things are put in subjection," it is evident that He is excepted who put all things in subjection to
Him. When all things are subjected to Him, then the Son
Himself also will be subjected to the One who subjected all
things to Him, so that God may be all in all.*

The comprehensiveness of that biblical teaching is absolutely
whole and unbroken. As we go through this text, it is clear that

all things are put by the Father under subjection to Jesus Christ, and Jesus Christ shall present all things to the Father, that God may be all in all.

That is the consummation. It is not about us—it is about God. More particularly, it is about the Father glorifying Himself in the Son, and the Son glorifying the Father in the purchased possession of the church, which is presented back to the Father spotless and without fault, that God may be all in all.

Christ is coming to rule, and in this rule—this active rule, this visible and unquestioned sovereignty—there will be the rising and the falling of nations. He will rule with a rod of iron. This is a comprehensive reign that includes all beings and all nations. Note that it is an eternal and universal reign. It includes the entire cosmos.

Christ is coming in reality; Christ is coming in authority; and Christ is coming *in judgment*. He will reign not only as king, but as judge. And as a judicious king, He will "execute judgment," as we are told in Jude 15.

Frighteningly, however, we live in a culture that takes as its motto, *No Fear*. We see this all around us. From media presentations to advertising campaigns, there is no fear. But not only is there no fear, neither is there any shame. We live in a society that no longer knows how to blush.

Sometime back I was on an episode of *Larry King Live*, debating the issue of homosexuality and homosexual marriage. One of the other guests on this program was Marianne Williamson, a New Age writer and pastor of the Unity Congregation in Detroit. I had just finished speaking of an objective morality and true Christian love, which requires that believers share the knowledge of God's verdict on homosexuality with homosexuals as an act of love. After all, the first act of true compassion is telling the truth. At that point, however, Marianne responded by saying, ". . . a God of love is much more important than a God of judgment or a God of fear."[8]

I will readily admit that she had the audience and I did not, but according to Scripture I had the truth and she did not. But what happened next was more interesting still. Before I had a chance to reply, a Jewish philosopher on the program made an astute observation. He responded to Ms. Williamson by saying, "I would like to make a statement on behalf of the God of judgment. I actually—if God were only loving and not judging I would have a very scary time. There is in fact a guy—the guy who does *Conversations with God*, the bestseller, who believes Hitler went to heaven. That's because he believes in an all loving God. I actually like a judging God."[9] That was very insightful on his part. While this gentleman did not understand the Gospel, he did understand that one cannot say God without saying Judge.

John Murray reminded us in *Redemption Accomplished and Applied* that we cannot set love and wrath apart as opposites, as if those are different functions.[10] Wrath is God's settled opposition to sin. We should remind ourselves that God's love is not a mushy sentimentality as in a theology copyrighted by Hallmark. Love has content. God's love is a holy love. And His holiness is a loving holiness.

Indeed, God's love is a discriminating love. Though that may be politically incorrect, the Bible will not let us see it any other way. God's love discriminates according to His holiness. If God did not pour out His wrath on the ungodly, He would not love in any genuine sense. If one loves all things, both good and evil, then one's love is not true love, but mere sentimentality.

We are told that when Christ comes, He will execute judgment. Second Corinthians 5:10 tells us, "For we must all appear before the judgment seat of Christ, so that each one may be compensated for his deeds in the body, according to what he has done, whether good or bad." Similarly, in Revelation 22:12 we read these words: "Behold, I am coming quickly, and My reward is with Me, to render to every man according to what he has done."

How, then, are we to live in light of Christ's glorious coming? And in the anticipation of His judgment, what should be our response?

Paul made this clear, preaching on Mars Hill (recorded in Acts 17:30-31), when he said, "Therefore having overlooked the times of ignorance, God is now declaring to men that all people everywhere should repent, because He has fixed a day in which He will judge the world in righteousness through a Man whom He has appointed, having furnished proof to all men, by raising Him from the dead."

So how did Paul clarify our proper response? Repentance. Living with the knowledge of the fact that Christ will glorify Himself in coming as judge, what should be our response but to repent of our sins? And what should be our proclamation to a dying world? Repent and believe on the Lord Jesus Christ. Knowing that this judgment is coming, all of life is transformed. It leads to a complete transformation of our thinking and our living.

Christ is coming in judgment. And in His coming, the sheep and the goats will be separated. In His coming, righteousness will be executed among the nations. In His coming, each will be compensated for his deeds in the body, whether good or bad.

Like the martyrs who cried out in Revelation 6:10, we too sometimes wonder how long the judgment will be delayed. Though we do not know when this judgment will come, we live in the knowledge that it is coming, surely and certainly.

Christ is coming in reality; Christ is coming in authority; Christ is coming in judgment; and Christ is coming *for redemption*. "Lift up your heads," we are told, "because your redemption is drawing near" (Luke 21:28). Too many evangelicals have not taken into account the reality that Christ's return is a part of salvation history. It is also the consummation of our redemption.

This, again, is clear from Hebrews 9:24-28:

For Christ did not enter a holy place made with hands, a mere
copy of the true one, but into heaven itself, now to appear in the
presence of God for us; nor was it that He would offer Himself
often, as the high priest enters the holy place year by year with
blood that is not his own. Otherwise, He would have needed to
suffer often since the foundation of the world; but now once
at the consummation of the ages He has been manifested to
put away sin by the sacrifice of Himself. And inasmuch as it is
appointed for men to die once and after this comes judgment,
so Christ also, having been offered once to bear the sins of
many, will appear a second time for salvation without reference
to sin, to those who eagerly await Him.

Two comings are described here. At the first coming, He came
with explicit reference to sin. When He came in Bethlehem, His
face was already pointed to Jerusalem, and there He shed His
blood for the remission of our sins. That, indeed, is the only sufficient sacrifice for our sins. There will be nothing else, nothing
added, nothing other.

In his commentary on Hebrews, John Calvin put it thus:

The Apostle urges this one thing,— that we ought not to be
disquieted by vain and impure longings for new kinds of expi-
ations, for the death of Christ is abundantly sufficient for us.
Hence, he says, that he once appeared and made a sacrifice to
abolish sins, and that at his second coming he will make openly
manifest the efficacy of his death, so that sin will have no more
power to hurt us.[11]

Calvin then concluded by speaking of this passage:

. . . in my judgment he intended to express something more suit-
able to his present purpose, namely, that Christ at his coming
will make it known how truly and really he had taken away
sins, so that there would be no need of any other sacrifice to
pacify God; as though he had said, "When we come to the tri-
bunal of Christ, we shall find that there was nothing wanting
in his death."[12]

In other words, all the peoples of the earth will see, in His coming, that He comes a second time for redemption. Moreover, when He comes, they will also understand why He came the first time, and so they will understand what He accomplished on the cross, even if they did not respond to Him in faith.

"He came to His own, and those who were His own did not receive Him. But as many as received Him, to them He gave the right to become children of God . . ." (John 1:11-12). Two comings, two revelations, one redemption. The first time He came with reference to sin. Now He comes without reference to sin, but so that those who eagerly await Him will see with all others that He accomplished salvation. Nothing can be added to it, and nothing can be taken from it.

John the Baptist said of Christ, "Behold, the Lamb of God who takes away the sin of the world!" (John 1:29). And in the book of Revelation, looking forward, we see the Lamb upon the throne. Christ, our High Priest, has accomplished our salvation, and we see that when He comes again, that salvation will be manifest to all, and the verdict will be written across all eternity. Christ is coming in redemption.

Lastly, Christ is coming *in glory*. Matthew 25:31-32 says, "But when the Son of Man comes in His glory, and all the angels with Him, then He will sit on His glorious throne. All the nations will be gathered before Him. . . ."

Now, think carefully about this. In His first coming, Christ came in glory, but that glory was veiled to the world of unbelief. We have already noted from John's Gospel that "He came to His own, and those who were His own did not receive Him" (John 1:11). John 1:14 clarifies for us that Christ did indeed come in glory in His first coming: "And the Word became flesh, and dwelt among us, and we saw His glory, glory as of the only begotten from the Father, full of grace and truth." But all did not see this glory in His first advent.

Compare that with the vision of Daniel 7, where we see the ultimate revelation, when all shall behold His glory.

> I kept looking in the night visions, and behold, with the clouds of heaven, one like a Son of Man was coming, and He came up to the Ancient of Days and was presented before Him. And to Him was given dominion, glory and a kingdom, that all the peoples, nations and men of every language might serve Him. His dominion is an everlasting dominion which will not pass away; and His kingdom is one which will not be destroyed.
>
> —vv. 13-14

If in His first coming His glory was veiled to the world of unbelief, when He comes the second time it will be manifest so that all shall see His glory. We wonder what this will look like. Looking at Revelation 4—5, we discover the magnificent throne language that is revealed there, and we see something of the vision of what is to come.

> Out from the throne come flashes of lightning and sounds and peals of thunder. And there were seven lamps of fire burning before the throne, which are the seven Spirits of God; and before the throne there was something like a sea of glass, like crystal; and in the center and around the throne, four living creatures full of eyes in front and behind. The first creature was like a lion, and the second creature like a calf, and the third creature had a face like that of a man, and the fourth creature was like a flying eagle. And the four living creatures, each one of them having six wings, are full of eyes around and within; and day and night they do not cease to say, "HOLY, HOLY, HOLY IS THE LORD GOD, THE ALMIGHTY, WHO WAS AND WHO IS AND WHO IS TO COME."
>
> —4:4-8

John continues reporting on this theme in Revelation 4:11, where the twenty-four elders are saying, "Worthy are You, our Lord and our God, to receive glory and honor and power;

for You created all things, and because of Your will they existed, and were created." He continues in a similar vein in Revelation 5:9-13:

> *And they sang a new song, saying, "Worthy are You to take the book and to break its seals; for You were slain, and purchased for God with Your blood men from every tribe and tongue and people and nation. You have made them to be a kingdom and priests to our God; and they will reign upon the earth." Then I looked, and I heard the voice of many angels around the throne and the living creatures and the elders; and the number of them was myriads of myriads, and thousands of thousands, saying with a loud voice, "Worthy is the Lamb that was slain to receive power and riches and wisdom and might and honor and glory and blessing." And every created thing which is in heaven and on the earth and under the earth and on the sea, and all things in them, I heard saying, "To Him who sits on the throne, and to the Lamb, be blessing and honor and glory and dominion forever and ever."*

Similarly, in Isaiah 6, Isaiah records his vision of the Lord as the tabernacle was filled with God's glory. And as he heard the declaration, Isaiah understood that "the whole earth is full of His glory." Indeed, we know that in Christ's coming, the whole cosmos shall be full of His glory.

Scripture directs us to await our redemption that draws nigh, to lift up our heads, and to understand that Christ's coming is the consummation of the ages. Christ's coming will declare our redemption that was for once for all accomplished. Christ's coming will establish His universal reign, manifested throughout all the cosmos. Indeed, Christ's coming is all about God's glory. The Son is glorified in His coming, and in His coming He glorifies the Father. So also the whole earth will be seen to be full of God's glory.

When the Lord returns, we will know this beyond question. His work of atonement is accomplished. Upon His return,

His coming with reference to sin will be fully manifested as having been accomplished. Sin will be atoned, death will be defeated, all things will be subjected, justice will be executed, righteousness will be established, every knee will be bowing, and every tongue will be confessing. There will be a new heaven and a new earth, and the saints will reign with God, that He may be all in all.

We know not the day or the hour, but we do have the assurance of His coming. We do know that the day of Christ's return is approaching. Consequently, we understand that history has a purpose. We recognize that the scales of justice will indeed be balanced. And we are strengthened by the awareness that Christ will come to claim His purchased possession. In faith we see that the blood of the martyrs will be vindicated. With confidence we understand that the dead in Christ shall rise. With anticipation we await the day when the saints will reign with him, and our vision is of the Lamb who shall rule from His throne.

As the book of Revelation comes to an end, and the canon of Scripture closes, we read these words: "He who testifies to these things says, 'Yes, I am coming quickly.' Amen. Come, Lord Jesus" (Rev. 22:20). May we, by God's grace, join the apostle John in praying, "Come, Lord Jesus."

NOTES

1. Frank Kermode, *The Sense of an Ending: Studies in the Theory of Fiction* (New York: Oxford University Press, 2000).

2. Neil Postman, *Amusing Ourselves to Death: Public Discourse in the Age of Show Business* (New York: Penguin, 1985).

3. Quoted from the *New American Standard Bible*. Unless otherwise noted, all biblical citations will be taken from the NASB.

4. Mark A. Noll, *The Scandal of the Evangelical Mind* (Grand Rapids, MI: Eerdmans, 1994).

5. As Francis Scheaffer spoke of the necessity of reaffirming "true truth," in the most incredible sense we live in an age in which I must insist I mean by this "real reality." After all, we live in a world that has come up with expressions like "virtual reality," which means that something is not but just passes for real.

6. Paul Davies, *The Last Three Minutes: Conjectures About the Ultimate Fate of the Universe* (New York: Basic Books, 1994).

7. Charles H. Spurgeon, "The Two Advents of Christ," in *The Metropolitan Tabernacle Pulpit*, Vol. 8 (Pasadena, TX: Pilgrim Publications, 1969; repr. 1985), p. 43.

8. Larry King Live Transcripts (on-line), from edition aired March 9, 2000, accessed at
   http://edition.cnn.com/TRANSCRIPTS/0003/09/lkl.00.html.
9. Ibid.
10. John Murray, *Redemption Accomplished and Applied* (Grand Rapids, MI: Eerdmans,
    1955).
11. John Calvin, *The Epistle of Paul the Apostle to the Hebrews*, in Vol. 22 of *Calvin's
    Commentaries*, ed. and trans. John Owen (Grand Rapids, MI: Baker, 1993), p. 219.
12. Ibid., p. 220.

8

THE BELIEVER'S PASSION FOR
THE GLORY OF CHRIST

JIM ELLIFF

I MET FRANCIS AND EDITH SCHAEFFER at their home in Huemoz, Switzerland, as a young ministerial student in the early 1970s. Over tea, Edith spoke passionately about "the tapestry" of their lives in Switzerland and their ministry to skeptics, called L'Abri. We then went with her to the Catholic town and canton that they had been forced to leave years earlier. In an old gray chapel Dr. Schaeffer preached the candlelight Christmas Eve service as he had been doing, returning every year but one, since they had been evicted from that area. I will never forget the thrill of seeing that sermon in print some time later, entitled "What Difference Has Looking Made?" from Luke 2.[1]

Like many reading these lines, I have been fascinated with the lives of the Schaeffers, not only for the "Schaeffer apologetic," which stands on its own, but perhaps even more so because of their passion for truth and their single-minded desire to see Christ honored in everything they did. How do we explain people like the Schaeffers who exuded so much of Christ in such a compelling manner?

Part of that passion can be seen in a seminal passage in Edith Schaeffer's first autobiographical work, *L'Abri*. The date was 1954, and they were returning to Switzerland after eighteen months in America. Out of the sentiments expressed here, they began the entirely new work called L'Abri, or in English "the shelter."

> We were going back with an expectation of something rather special, with an excitement to see what "God will do." We had done quite a lot of thinking and self-examining over the previous few years. It seemed to us that so much of Christianity was being spread by advertising designed to "put across" something, and that there was very little genuine recognition of the existence of the supernatural work of the Holy Spirit. One morning at Chalet Bijou's breakfast table, Fran had said to me, "Supposing we had awakened today to find everything concerning the Holy Spirit and prayer removed from the Bible—that is, not removed the way liberals would remove it, but that God had somehow really removed everything about prayer and the Holy Spirit from the Bible. What difference would it make *practically* between the way we worked yesterday and the way we would work today, and tomorrow? What difference would it make in the majority of Christians' practical work and plans? Aren't most plans laid out ahead of time? Isn't much work done by human talent, energy and clever ideas? Where does the supernatural power of God have a *real* place?"[2]

By seeking to become a living illustration of the power of God, the Schaeffers, over the next decades, would literally live out the passion of the apostle Paul—to glorify Christ by every means possible. It is this single-minded devotion to glorify Christ in the totality of life that made them so truly engaging and continually useful. I want to ask you a simple but straightforward question: "Do you have such a goal?"

Many noble goals have been scratched out on the backs of envelopes or on yellow pads or carefully written out in journals.

But why is it that these goals are not yet being accomplished? Why, in many instances, are they almost completely forgotten? An encompassing goal, such as we will explore, will not be accomplished without passion, and there will never be passion until you have an arresting value. What, to put it simply, is the benefit that fuels the passion behind the accomplishment of your goal? It is my aim to clarify Paul's supreme goal and the value that motivated it in such a way that we will be compelled to adopt it as our own.

I do not think it is news to you when I say that the apostle Paul was a man of large and numerous aspirations. He plainly had the goal of preaching the Gospel where Christ was not named, and to "know him and the power of his resurrection, and ... [to] share his sufferings, becoming like him in his death" (Phil. 3:10). Furthermore, he longed to "present everyone mature in Christ" (Col. 1:28). And in yet another place he sums up his goals by adding, "I have fought the good fight, I have finished the race, I have kept the faith" (2 Tim. 4:7). And these are only a sampling of his objectives.

To grasp the statement we are about to analyze (1:20), we need to remember that the apostle is in prison in Rome for his faith when he writes these words. He seems to expect deliverance soon, typical of his indefatigable optimism and sense of obligation to continue his labors for the church. He plans to continue to rejoice whatever the decision of the court concerning his case. His optimism fits his goal. I zoom into Paul's passion in the middle of a sentence, where we read: "as it is my eager expectation and hope that I will not be at all ashamed, but that with full courage now as always Christ will be honored in my body" (1:20).

If you pare away all of the qualifiers, you find that the apostle Paul is saying this: In nothing ashamed; in everything magnifying Christ. That phrase I take to be the passion of his life.

IN NOTHING ASHAMED

"I will not be at all ashamed." Paul is declaring, "I do not want to preach boldly and then live fearfully. I do not want to boast in God and then trust in myself. I do not want to command obedience from other people and then fumble around in disobedience in my own life. I do not want to declare publicly the Lord Jesus Christ but then deny Him privately. I do not want to begin well and end like a fool. I do not want to be a defector."

One of the great figures in martyrdom during the English Reformation was Thomas Cranmer. He died in the same period of time as Hugh Latimer and Nicholas Ridley. You may remember their inspiring stories. Cranmer was the archbishop in England, but because of his efforts at reform, when Bloody Mary began her reign, he was clearly a candidate for martyrdom. At first he stood his ground firmly. He was thrown into a dark and damp prison. His fingers were scraped and made raw by his accusers. Remember those hands, for they shall be heard of again.

When he would not recant by deprivation, they changed their strategy and put him in the posh residence of an Oxford dean. They decided to try to break him by pouring out kindness and civil appeals on him. In such a vulnerable moment, contrary to all he had previously suffered, he actually recanted.

He took a piece of paper and signed a statement to this effect: "I, Thomas Cranmer, late bishop of Canterbury, do renounce all heresies and errors not in agreement with the Church of Rome. I acknowledge the pope as the supreme head of the church, whom all must obey. I believe in the seven sacraments, purgatory, and prayers to the saints. I am sorry that I ever thought otherwise and led others away from the Church of Rome." With his own hand, which had been scraped earlier, he signed the statement.

Mary insisted on his death anyway. St. Mary's Church overflowed with spectators who came to hear the old archbishop give his endorsement of the Catholic Church before his death.

When it came his time to speak, Cranmer first knelt and prayed out loud to the Lord. He then stood up, and among other things that he said about care for the poor and love for one another, he spoke these words: "And now I come to the great thing which troubles my conscience more than anything I ever did in my whole life. I now renounce the things written with my hand against the truth in my heart. I feared death, I wrote the recantation to save my life, and because my hand has offended, writing against my heart, therefore my hand shall be punished first, for when I come to the fire, it shall be burned first. And as for the pope, I refuse him, as Christ's enemy with all his false doctrines."

They led him up to be burned, among the jeers of the people. As the fire began to burn, he stretched out his right hand and said, "This unworthy right hand, this hand has offended!" He thrust that hand into the fire first, and soon he died.

What the apostle Paul expresses with great fervor and depth of emotion is, in my amplification, something like this: "I do not want to be one of them. I do not want to be a person who preaches to others and then is disqualified for the prize. In nothing do I want to be ashamed before my God or before His people."

I often pray that way. I have known too many defectors from the Christian ranks. Just recently three more Christian leaders here in the U.S. have experienced some awful sin in their lives and now struggle mightily, ashamed before God and the church. Thankfully, there is forgiveness for those who repent, and there is love from the people of God, but the losses they have suffered are huge. I do not want to become a moral defector, but I know it is possible. And so I pray. In fact, I have often prayed something like this: "Lord, let me finish well. Please let me die well." As Robertson McQuilkin penned so hauntingly in his poem by the same name, "Lord, let me get home before dark."[3]

IN EVERYTHING MAGNIFYING CHRIST

What else is there in this goal of Paul's? The positive side of his passion is this: It was his expectation and his aspiration that Christ would be *magnified in his body*.

Every great person of God thinks like this. Read their biographies, and you will find this kind of yearning on page after page. They longed and believed that the greatest good of all was Jesus Christ, and that for Christ to be magnified through their mortal flesh was all that ultimately mattered. They would give everything for that.

You see this passion in John the Baptist. Some disciples of John come to him and say, "Rabbi, he who was with you across the Jordan, to whom you bore witness—look, he is baptizing, and all are going to him" (John 3:26). Despite John the Baptist's unconventional taste in clothing and cuisine, he was an immensely successful man. People had come to him from the whole region to be baptized. Many of our contemporaries would feel quite exceptional, with baptisms on the rise and people flocking to hear their messages. However, at precisely this point in his popularity his disciples come to him and report, "All are going to him [Jesus]."

What does John the Baptist think about this? Does he secretly resent the fact that people are beginning to go to another preacher in town? Does he rally his followers to keep his leadership of the large numbers? No; rather he says, "The one who has the bride is the bridegroom. The friend of the bridegroom, who stands and hears him, rejoices greatly at the bridegroom's voice. Therefore this joy of mine is now complete" (3:29). And then he gives us that most memorable line: "He must increase, but I must decrease" (v. 30). In other words, "All I am is a torch that casts light on Jesus Christ at the beginning of His public ministry, and then I am gone—that's it. It's all about Christ—it's not about me."

If you will ever be usable as a man or woman in the kingdom

of God, you will need to have that spirit, and you will need to have it deeply rooted in your heart. I long to be able to say consistently, "What I really care about is not how well I do, not how good I look, not how the statistics look, not even how things look to my peers. I long that Christ would be magnified, that He would increase."

When we magnify Christ, we do not make Him any bigger. When you magnify something, you are simply making it larger to the eye. Christ cannot be made any bigger or more glorious than He already is. But like the Hubble telescope, we go out to display the attractiveness and magnificence of Christ.

Do you long to do that? All your other goals may be very important, but this has to be supreme. If you miss it here, you have missed it all.

There is a compelling passage in 2 Corinthians 4 that addresses this magnification of Christ to others. Here Paul is describing this idea even more fully and eloquently. He says, "And even if our gospel is veiled, it is veiled only to those who are perishing" (v. 3). What do those without Christ need? They need their blindness removed by the light of the good news of the glory of God in the person of Jesus Christ.

Paul continues:

> For what we proclaim is not ourselves, but Jesus Christ as Lord, with ourselves as your servants for Jesus' sake. For God, who said, "Let light shine out of darkness," has shone in our hearts to give the light of the knowledge of the glory of God in the face of Jesus Christ.
>
> —vv. 5-6

Paul claims that light is what His hearers need, and thus this is what he preaches—the glory of Christ. But how does this happen? He reveals the method in the next several verses:

> But we have this treasure in jars of clay, to show that the surpassing power belongs to God and not to us. We are

*afflicted in every way, but not crushed; perplexed, but not
driven to despair; persecuted, but not forsaken; struck down,
but not destroyed; always carrying in the body the death of
Jesus, so that the life of Jesus may also be manifested in our
bodies.*

—vv. 7-10

Then he concludes, "So death is at work in us, but life in you"
(v. 12). Just as in the Philippians passage, it is the *glory of Christ*
that is the central issue in Paul's mind-set. The light of the glory
of Christ has come into our lives. We have Christ; we are His.
We preach Christ; we do not preach ourselves. These bodies carry
this gift to others. But here is the striking thing to notice here:
There is some connection between weakness in us and the manifestation of the glory of Christ in our lives. As we give our bodies over to whatever is necessary for the proclamation of the
Gospel and for sacrificial obedience to Jesus Christ, the glory of
Christ begins to radiate through us and becomes read and understood by people who are in our churches and around us. I do
not fully understand the mystery of this connection, I freely
admit, but I believe I can see the principle at work. Though two
believers may say identical things about Christ, there is an unmis-
takable peculiarity (are we not to be "a peculiar people," 1 Pet.
2:9, KJV?) in the one whose singular desire is to magnify Christ
at any cost.

THE INTENSIFYING OF THE GOAL

To understand Paul's goal, which will hopefully be our goal as well,
I removed the qualifying words and phrases and expressed this goal
in its simplest form: In nothing ashamed; in everything magnifying Christ. But now let's add the qualifiers to bring texture back
to the goal, like a painter who shades and lightens to make his
painting three-dimensional rather than merely one-dimensional.

Paul says, first of all, that this goal is his *"eager* expectation"
(Phil. 1:20). This means Paul is dead serious about accomplish-

ing this goal. He is, simply stated, consumed by it. The man of faith George Muller of Bristol, England, was a man of similar earnestness. As you may recall, Muller was notable not only for his faith, but also for his consistency with God. He was used by God to feed, clothe, and house over 10,000 orphans over his life span without asking anybody but God for the means to do this work. His life goal was to magnify Christ. Once he was asked the secret of his service for God. He answered, all the time leaning over further and further until his torso was almost parallel to the ground:

> There was a day when I died, utterly died—died to George Muller, his opinions, preferences, tastes and will—died to the world, its approval or censure—died to the approval or blame even of my brethren and friends—and since then I have studied only to show myself approved unto God.

Such is the earnestness that we need. Charles Spurgeon said that praying without this is like hunting with a dead dog. I once knew a lay couple whose desire to magnify Christ was so earnest and real (though they were people of modest gifts) that the magnetism created from the mixture of desire with real human limitations was easily the most attractive element of the entire congregation of which they were a part. This church perhaps experienced more of Christ than any other I have witnessed. The effect of the lives of these two people has been felt for over twenty-five years. It is so great that no one could properly estimate it.

Paul uses the words "expectation" and "hope." They show optimism for reaching the goal. But this implication is also important: His desire sometimes falls short of the reality. The words "eager expectation" come from the concept of straining the neck forward. He presses toward his goal. He has an expectation of its fulfillment. But not even Paul fully arrives at this goal while on earth. There is something to be said, however, for the optimistic continuance of a person who has this goal firmly in his or her heart, even when there is failure. Edith Schaeffer spoke to this when she wrote:

> L'Abri had started! What were our "visions" or "expecta-tions" or "goals"? Simply a desire to demonstrate the exis-tence of God by our lives and our work. Had Fran become a "perfect" person now? Had his quick temper been conquered never to rear its head again? Would he never do anything in his own strength again, and perfectly live by prayer, moment by moment? Was I now going to have no faults? Would all my decisions, moment by moment, be the Lord's decisions? Would I really be "dead to self" all the time, and have no frustra-tions as I cooked, weeded gardens, and washed dishes for an endless stream of people? Did we have a sense of having "arrived"? No, a million times *no*. But, God is very patient and gentle with His children, as in a real measure (only He knows the ingredients of sincerity and honesty) they attempt to live in close communication with Him, asking for help, asking for strength, depending on His wisdom and power rather than on their own cleverness and zip![4]

Notice, furthermore, that Paul says, "It is my eager expecta-tion and hope that I will not be *at all* ashamed" (1:20a). This aspiration is inclusive of all aspects of his life. There is no com-partmentalizing of life by Paul. There is no Sunday spirituality or Monday morning retreat from the pursuit of this goal.

Again, you must remember that Paul wrote these words while in prison. In prison you might expect him to have some right to complain and dichotomize by saying, "This is not my public min-istry. This is a time where I am just going to have to suffer, and I can say and be what I want to be." No; rather he thinks, "I do not—even in this place, even if nobody is looking but God—I do not want to be ashamed before my God."

But then he goes on, "It is my eager expectation and hope that I will not be at all ashamed, but that *with full courage* now as always Christ will be honored in my body, whether by life or by death" (1:20). This goal not only covers all things, but it requires *"full courage."* He intends, with God giving him grace, to live out his life not in halves, not holding back, but with courage. There is an aggressive forthrightness to this life. This courage includes not only his speech, but his bearing, his demeanor, his whole way of living his life. He will have to stand with courage even when no one else will stand with him.

Then notice further that he says, "It is my eager expectation and hope that I will not be at all ashamed, but that with full courage *now as always Christ will* be honored in my body." The goal is not only all-consuming and all-encompassing, demanding all boldness, but it is *"now as always."* As it *always* has been—when things were better, and things were perhaps easier—but *now* as well, up to and including this current situation in prison. When we are young, eager Christians and when we are old Christians, it must be the same. When everyone has left us (as they did Paul, who described his experience at the end of 2 Timothy), and when everybody loves us—at all times this goal applies.

What a disheartening thing it is to see an older brother or sister give up and set his or her life on cruise control for the rest of the way. Always, *always* you are to be about this great aspiration in life. You must stir up and maintain your passion for the glory of Christ.

My father-in-law has the interesting habit of turning off his car engine and coasting the last few feet into his garage. But spiritually you must never turn off your engine and try to glide into home. Some of us who are a bit younger have to see that you make it. I am sometimes absolutely amazed when I think about how few older men are really going on with God, including some who have been in the ministry and leadership all their lives. Why is it that they do not press on with God? They once were as zealous as I am. That is the frightening thing. What happened?

Then notice Paul's statement at the end of this verse: "It is my eager expectation and hope that I will not be at all ashamed, but that with full courage now as always Christ will be honored in my body, *whether by life or by death*" (1:20). The goal is to employ all circumstances, by means of life and even death. Whatever the circumstances, this goal still stands. Christ was not only glorified through many years of service in the apostle Paul's life, but also by means of his death. It should be our ambition that Christ would be magnified in our bodies, but we do not have the final say as to how that will actually happen.

THE VALUE FUELING THE PASSION

How do you get to a point in your life where you want this goal? How do you have that kind of aspiration when people are not looking at you, as well as when people are looking? What ignites the passions and causes us to pay the ultimate price? I believe you cannot have the apostle's goal without the apostle's value.

Not long ago my family and I were in Canada and went to see Niagara Falls. The place we liked best was by the river just above the falls, exactly where the water plummets straight down. At this point you are just a few feet above the top of the falls.

If my wife were leaning over the edge and dropped her diamond ring down into the water, guess what I would do? *Nothing*! I would not dive in for it because it is not worth it. It's a few hundred dollars worth of diamond, but it's absolutely not worth it, as far as I'm concerned. But if my little girl or one of my boys dropped over the edge, I would almost unthinkingly risk my life to try and save him or her. Why would I do something so dangerous that would almost certainly mean my own death? I would do this and more only because of the immense value of those children to me.

We all have values that drive us, shaping our goals and consuming our passions. What fills your thoughts and occupies your "high places"? Many of us have contented ourselves with far less than fellowship with Christ. But when the apostle states his highest value, he does not quibble over secondary matters.

Years ago I took my wife and son on an extended preaching tour of South Africa. On one occasion we were passing one of the most alluring sites in the world—the Table Mountain in Cape Town. As we drove by, I attempted to get my preschool child to look at this stunning site, but he was occupied with a plastic toy worth only a few cents. I was totally unsuccessful. He was completely happy with the toy and would not trade his enjoyment of the toy for one of the truly great vistas any person could ever be permitted to visually enjoy. He had exchanged something of immense value for something worth almost nothing. When it comes to Christ, some are perfectly happy with such things as activities in the youth department or happy songs in the service or a few dollars in the bank while the greatest value of all, fellowship with Christ, is totally neglected.

For some reason many believers live poorly, exert themselves weakly, and fumble around foolishly, but why? The only reason I can detect is this: We do not have a benefit before us that has the ability to engender noble activity. The apostle's value is found in the words immediately following Philippians 1:20: "For to me [as if he is saying, "This is the reason I live for this goal; this is the reason and the rationale that causes me to be so intense about every single aspect of my life and my ministry]—to live is Christ, and to die is gain" (v. 21). He is articulating in this profound set of words the simple fact that while living on earth we enjoy the preciousness of true communion with Christ; and dying augments that same joy by bringing us unclouded and unstoppable fellowship with Christ in heaven. That is the value that will call forth something from us that is way beyond the normal and will propel us toward the goal of glorifying Christ.

William Burns, the tool that God used along with Robert Murray M'Cheyne in the revival of Dundee, Scotland, in the nineteenth century, was later commissioned to go to China for the sake of the Gospel. When he was leaving by ship, he reflected on the cost. "Why am I not, as many, going forth in search of mammon; or put to sea, as some are, because they are unprofitable even in man's account on land? Who maketh thee to differ? O! to live under the full influence of Christ's constraining love! To us to live will thus be Christ, and to us to die will be gain."[5]

When believers have the immense value of Christ in their minds and understand something of fellowship with Christ and the beauty of Christ and the largeness and loveliness of Christ, they will not only go to China, but even to the stake. The history of Christianity bears this out in a plethora of cases. We will do anything if the value of the love of Christ is kept continually before us. Knowing Christ purifies and focuses all of life. If the highest value is communion with Him, then we will never wish to live shamefully before Him and will always long to display His beauty to others.

Interestingly, we will also find that the goal and the value have a reciprocal effect on each other. Going forward toward the higher goal will become yet another means of enjoying fellowship with Christ, and vice versa. Paul not only sought to know Christ—he longed to "share his sufferings, becoming like him in his death" (3:10). The value of knowing Christ pushes us on to the higher goal of seeking His glory in all things; and seeking the magnification of Christ in the totality of life, even with the accompanying suffering, provides sweetness of fellowship ("[that I] may share his sufferings") unknown on any other plane. Deep calls unto deep. For this reason, when the value of fellowship with Christ is ahead of us, the direction we are headed will ultimately be the happiest of all directions.

When we believers see the immense value of Jesus Christ, we

have a bit of a struggle about whether we want to be in heaven with Christ or here on earth. This will be especially true as we experience the limitations of the body through sickness, old age, or suffering. And this is the point to which the apostle comes in his explanation. He says that he does not know whether it is best to be in heaven or to be on the earth. "I am hard pressed between the two. My desire is to depart and be with Christ, for that is far better. But to remain in the flesh is more necessary on your account" (1:23-24).

I think there is something very revealing about us when we examine whether we really would like to be there as opposed to remaining here. It tells us something about where our highest value really is. The apostle Paul saw such a supreme value in Christ that he would honestly rather be in heaven with Him than here. Will we say that when the time comes?

Howell Harris, an itinerant evangelist and one of the early leaders of the Evangelical Awakening in Wales, expressed what longing for more of Christ does to one's concept of death. He said on his deathbed:

> I feel my spirit leaving all places and men here below, and going to my Father, and to my native country, home, yea my own home. And though I am here below in His kingdom, yet whilst I wait to be called home, my longings and cries are insatiable indeed. And when the Lord of glory answers me that I shall soon go to Him, my spirit does so burn with love to that dear Saviour that I flee to Him and can take no denial. I can't stay here, and though I am but a bit of dust and nothing before Thee, yet O Father, may I without offending Thee ask this one special favour: O Saviour, give me leave, though a worm, to ask without offending that my time be shortened. . . . This is Thy lower house, and Thou art my life and all here below; That is Thy upper house, and Thou art gone before me, and therefore I must come. Thou can'st not leave me long; Thou art both here and there also my heaven. . . . All that others have in this world, and in religion, and in themselves, I have in Thee—pleasures, and riches, safety, hon-

our, life, righteousness, holiness, wisdom, bliss, joy, gaiety, and happiness. . . . And if a child longs for his father, a traveler for the end of his journey, a workman to finish his work, a prisoner for his liberty, an heir for the full possession of his estate; so in all these respects I cannot help longing to go home.[6]

Without the value of fellowship with Christ in the first place in the hierarchy of our affections, we will not be able to sing with Isaac Watts, "Were the whole realm of nature mine, that were a present far too small. Love so amazing, so divine, demands my life, my soul, my all."

Does the lack of fellowship with Christ explain why so many true Christians are lifeless and faltering and unmotivated in our time? Can our failure to treasure communion with Him be the reason for such paltry living and such listlessness and aimlessness among so many otherwise genuine believers? And if that is so, will you seek to regain the sense of treasure that is to be found in fellowship with Christ?

Once more, in an amplified or expanded manner, I want to restate the apostle's goal—both his value and passion. I do this in hope that you might fully adopt, not only his language, but his heart:

This is my resolute goal, my impassioned ambition, my eager expectation, and what I strain forward to accomplish, that in not one aspect of life, public or private, comfortable or difficult, shall I be ashamed or found dishonorable and conscience-stricken, but with all boldness, aggressiveness, and winsome outspokenness, in both speech and demeanor, I will at all times, even when old or in difficult straits, magnify, amplify, or make larger to the eyes and ears of others Christ Himself, by whatever means He sees fit, whether by life or by death. For this supreme value compels me—life is only found in fellowship with Him and is no living at all without that fellowship, and dying is to know more of Him in unbroken and unfiltered communion forever in heaven.

NOTES

1. Francis Schaeffer, *No Little People, No Little Places*, from *The Complete Works of Francis Schaeffer*, Vol. 3 (Wheaton, IL: Crossway Books, 1982), pp. 121-133.
2. Edith Schaeffer, *L'Abri* (Wheaton, IL: Tyndale House, 1969), pp. 64-65.
3. Robertson McQuilkin, "Let Me Get Home Before Dark," Columbia International, http://www.ciu.edu/articles/gethome.htm.
4. Edith Schaeffer, *The Tapestry* (Waco, TX: Word, 1981), pp. 432-433.
5. Michael McMullen, *God's Polished Arrow* (Fearn, Scotland: Christian Focus Publications, 2000), pp. 103-104.
6. Hugh J. Hughes, *The Life of Howell Harris, the Welsh Reformer* (Hanley, England: Tentmaker Publications, 1996, reprint of 1892 edition), pp. 374-375.

INDEX